SALES NEGOTIATING
HANDBOOK

SALES NEGOTIATING HANDBOOK

Robert E. Kellar

PRENTICE HALL
Englewood Cliffs, New Jersey 07632

Prentice-Hall International, Inc., *London*
Prentice-Hall of Australia, Pty. Ltd., *Sydney*
Prentice-Hall Canada, Inc., *Toronto*
Prentice-Hall of India Private Ltd., *New Delhi*
Prentice-Hall of Japan, Inc., *Tokyo*
Prentice-Hall of Southeast Asia Pte. Ltd., *Singapore*
Editora Prentice-Hall do Brasil Ltda., *Rio de Janeiro*
Prentice-Hall Hispanoamericana, S.A., *Mexico*

© 1988 *by*

PRENTICE-HALL, INC.

Englewood Cliffs, N.J.

10 9 8 7 6 5 4 3 2 1

Library of Congress Cataloging-in-Publication Data

Kellar, Robert E.
  Sales negotiating handbook.

  Bibliography: p.
  Includes index.
  1. Selling. 2. Negotiation in business. I. Title.
HF5438.25.K44 1988   658.8'1   87-29172
ISBN 0-13-788100-2
ISBN 0-13-788092-8 (pbk.)

ISBN 0-13-788100-2
ISBN 0-13-788092-8 {PBK}

PRENTICE HALL
BUSINESS & PROFESSIONAL DIVISION
A division of Simon & Schuster
Englewood Cliffs, New Jersey 07632

How Using These Skills Will Multiply Your Sales Payoff

The moment you are given the discretion to grant (or to ask for) any kinds of concessions to your buyers you are in the role of negotiator. Since there are so many hidden areas of concession—like terms of sale, delivery, specifications, and dozens of others—where profits are impacted "right off the top," it becomes critical for you to exercise a whole new set of skills, above and beyond the basic selling skills. That's what this book is about.

Throughout these 11 chapters you will learn the skills, the discipline, and the easy-to-follow systems in each of the three stages of a sales negotiation. In Chapters 1-7 you will learn the fundamental steps in planning and preparing for a sales negotiation. In Chapters 8-10 you will learn the basic elements to be dealt with during the face-to-face bargaining stage of negotiation, and in Chapter 11, the critical follow-through skills which will enhance your profit margins and set the stage for future negotiations.

In a special section, I have included a comprehensive checklist summarizing many of the key points discussed throughout the book.

Salespeople often ask, "Why do I need this set of skills? My job is to sell." For the past several years many buying organizations throughout the world have been teaching their engineers, purchasing agents, and middle managers systematic ways to negotiate more profitable deals with their vendors. Some sales organizations have attempted to meet this challenge, but there is far too little material available to the sales professional specifically designed to improve sales negotiating skills.

The skills described in this text are designed specifically to help you improve not just sales volume, but net profit margin on each sale made. Using these skills will not only help you to achieve the best possible deal, but also provide you ways of doing that without causing win-lose results with your buyers.

Throughout these sales negotiating processes I have described methods of give-and-take so that the tradeoffs you arrive at with your buyers can usually result in a feeling of benefit to both sides.

If you are a seller of anything, these tools provide a systematic way of assuring that all the important bases have been covered and that others in your organization, who are important to the outcomes of your negotiations, have been included in a team effort approach. The bigger the stakes in the negotiation the greater the payoff in using these systematic practices.

The skills, the disciplines, and the simplified systems described are easily used by any sales representative in a wide variety of seller-buyer relationships. Sales managers should find these processes helpful, not only in improving results of individual salespeople, but also in building the team relationships so often overlooked in day-to-day negotiating. I am frequently reminded by sales professionals that the real culprits in "blowing" negotiations with buyers are higher management who inadvertently make concessions without taking time for adequate briefing—thus, the insights in this book might be profitably absorbed by executive levels as well. And, finally, these ideas could even benefit those buyers who could profit from a better understanding of the win-win potential of a more rational set of negotiating processes.

In fact, anybody who buys or sells anything would probably have better working relationships, while getting more profitable results, using these ideas.

The personal benefits to you, the sales professional, will come in many forms. Your personal income, immediate or long term, your esteem in an organization, your promotability, your working relationships, and your self-satisfaction are all bound to be improved.

This book has been written specifically for the sales professional, and in that respect is distinct from the majority of the literature written on the general subject of negotiating effectiveness. Throughout the text I have included easy-to-use formats and planning devices for applying the techniques described. Those salespeople who in the past have used these simple but vital negotiating tools have invariably achieved not only more sales but more profitable sales and more effective buyer relationships.

Use of these techniques, combined with your other natural selling skills, will add another level of depth to your sales professionalism. More importantly, it will add to your net results, by providing a framework with which to plan and conduct every sales agreement in which there are potential areas for tradeoff, whenever the buyer presses for concessions at any level or on any aspect of the sale.

Robert E. Kellar

Table of Contents

1

CONDUCTING EFFECTIVE SALES NEGOTIATIONS

Buyer: "Your price is too high."
Seller: "Where are you getting these units now?"
Buyer: "We get them from Vermont for 20 cents less than your quote."
Seller: "These from Vermont don't seem to be color-coded."
Buyer: "We don't need them color-coded."

(Note: It costs the seller 25 cents to color code.)

Seller: "What coding do you need?"
Buyer: "We stamp a three-digit code on them."

(Note: It would cost the seller two cents to stamp a three-digit code.)

Seller: "How much does that cost you?"
Buyer: "I don't know, but it's a pain—slows us down."
Seller: "We can lower our price by ten cents and give you the three digit-code."
Buyer: "You're on. We'll take 10,000 as soon as you can deliver."

EFFECTIVE SALES NEGOTIATIONS

The importance of negotiating effectively in our competitive world of business is so critical that organizations literally rise and fall on the fortunes of both formal and informal sales negotiations. The significance of the negotiator of effective sales agreements is probably underrated in many business firms. In terms of complexity, psychology, and skills required, negotiating goes well beyond the process of day-to-day selling.

To be an effective negotiator you certainly use many of the same skills required in the standard selling process. You need at least the same depth of knowledge, the persuasion skills, the disciplines and positive attitudes needed to be an effective sales professional. But in addition you must have an awareness of the process of "give and take" that so frequently goes on, particularly when larger stakes are involved. When the sale involves a range of complexities beyond a simple buying decision and when the decision involves commitments at different points throughout the organization, give-and-take must occur. Each year buying organizations are becoming more and more sophisticated in the bargaining processes posing a greater demand on the negotiating skills of today's sales professionals.

One of the most critical elements in successful negotiations involves the commitment you make to yourself in terms of goals, frequently referred to as your "aspiration level." This becomes a particularly important consideration when the negotiation is a team effort and several individuals must be committed to a high, but realistic, goal or outcome. In larger negotiations millions of dollars are at stake, and the difference of one or two percentage points one way or the other can translate into several thousands of dollars. In case after case, organizations fail to achieve anything near the full potential results in major negotiations simply because they do not set their sights high enough.

The art of negotiating seems to be practiced with more vigor in many parts of the world than in the United States. In both business and government we have frequently been outbargained seemingly due more to our failure to appreciate the nature of the negotiating process rather than any weakness in our bargaining position. The negotiation process is as old a practice as the conduct of business itself, probably originating with the early cave man who wished to barter tools and weapons for food and shelter at a mutually agreeable exchange. In our society, negotiating has been viewed by many as a win-lose process whereby one party often takes unfair advantage of the other through various devious means. This is not the essence of the negotiation process as practiced in healthy business relationships today. On the contrary, it is a means of arriving at a win-win outcome for both parties.

Unfortunately, when one side fails to do its homework or fails to learn the necessary skills, it can indeed fail to achieve a win-win outcome. Despite all the scientific systems we employ today in the conduct of business, the success or failure of negotiations often boils down to the human element. The strength of conviction, the bargaining skills, the tenacity of the personalities pitted face-to-face, more often than not determine the results of the negotiations. Not that the effective gathering of detailed information is anything less than critical to a complex negotiation, but of equal importance is the skill with which you, the negotiator, conduct yourself or your team in moving the bargaining process in a desired direction.

Negotiating: An Art or a Science

A salesman is on the verge of closing a deal with a customer for a $20,000 piece of machinery. The purchasing engineer asks for a 2% discount in addition to the 5% he is confident of getting anyway. There is a long pause, some calculating, and the salesman concedes. He really wants to close this sale. Before they are finished, the buyer has managed to get $300 worth of spare parts, $50 worth of technical manuals, and 90 days credit extended beyond the normal terms. Each time the salesman made a concession, the buyer asked for something in addition—and got it. The salesman made no counter-offers because each request seemed "reasonable." And, after all, he did make the sale.

An effective salesman? Perhaps. An effective negotiator? No. This salesman may be the highest volume producer around. But his impact on profits could be very marginal.

The moment you as the salesperson are given the authority to make concessions you assume a new and broader role. You are now a negotiator, and how well you perform that role can vitally affect the health of your organization.

In the case we have just described, the salesman had done a superb job of preparing for the sale. He had done his homework, had developed the need and desire to buy in the customer's mind, had made an excellent presentation, had probed for useful information, had overcome all objections and resistance raised, and had led very smoothly into an almost automatic close. But despite his thorough cost analysis, and attention to technical detail, and effective use of selling skills, when the chips were down he sacrificed over 50% of the potential net profits because he failed to negotiate effectively.

Time and Effort

Not all sales negotiations are as simple and straightforward as the one described above. Team negotiations involving several people on both sides are frequently employed in larger and more complex sales, or in licensing or distributorship types of bargaining situations. Sadly, but all too often, these negotiations are entered into haphazardly and are only superficially thought through. Although face-to-face negotiating skills are extremely important, as we saw above, there is no substitute for the time and effort required for effective preparation.

One of the greatest lessons we can learn from the great football coaches, the great orchestra conductors, and the great trial lawyers is their unwavering attention to preparation. Football, music, and trials are experiences of emotions—built on a base of preparation. Negotiating is an exercise in human interactions—built on a base of preparation.

Characteristics of Effective Negotiators

None of the characteristics of an effective negotiator are in conflict with those basic skills of an effective sales professional. There are, however, some different perspectives and emphases. For example, in major negotiations we are often dealing with much larger organizational issues, systems, and plans, frequently involving a "team" of individuals drawn from sales, engineering, cost accounting, and the like. This suggests a broader set of skills required by the negotiating team leader. The following five areas of characteristics generally address those traits that have been found to be of most importance:

Goal Orientation

To be an effective negotiator we need a high level of intrinsic motivation to set and achieve high performance targets. A willingness to take reasonable risk is an essential ingredient in this achievement motivation. We will be more effective negotiators if our confidence and patience prevails over pressures from either our own organization, or the other side, to lower our goals too readily as the negotiation proceeds.

Preparation

The combination of knowledge plus anticipation enables us to plan more effective negotiating targets, strategies, and tactics. The more information we can gather in a systematic way, about each element in our own product, systems, costs, and the people (as well as about the other side), the better able we are to plan—and planning is the keystone of successful preparation. Good planning involves in-depth probing, and often some internal negotiating, with people in our own organization. Learning everything possible about the strengths and weaknesses of each key influencer, on both sides of the negotiation, is a vital step in preparing and determining the attitude and "climate" we need to establish early-on in the face-to-face bargaining.

Skills

When the head-to-head maneuvers begin, there are certain fundamental skill characteristics any good negotiator needs. First, we need to grasp quickly the difference between real bargaining strengths versus assumed strengths on both sides. We need the ability to express ourselves clearly and to think clearly under pressure. We also need to have a feel for how far to bend, especially when the situation is not clearly defined. And most important, we must have confidence and self-esteem as well as an ability to gain the respect of the other party. There are six skills areas which are generally required in all face-to-face negotiating situations:

1. Making the opening offer (or demand).
2. Gathering and using new information during the discussions.
3. Establishing a credibility or legitimacy in the eyes of other party(s).
4. Employing effective tactics to control the situation.
5. Using effective counter-tactics.
6. Gaining a desirable commitment.

Follow-Through

Since the whole concept of negotiation suggests that both sides may be modifying their original proposals, we need to assure that anybody affected by the modifications be brought into the picture. There are three areas to attend to following the handshake and signatures that conclude the formal negotiation:

1. Documenting the details of the agreement.

2. Defining and clarifying all modifications.

3. Building on the relationship for future negotiations.

Despite all the attention given to documenting meticulous detail, the success of many negotiations frequently rests on the "good faith" of the negotiating parties to carry out the commitments commensurate with the spirit of the formal (and informal) agreements. Thus, time and effort at communicating and clarifying post-bargaining activities is an essential ingredient in the total negotiation process.

Perspective

There are many varieties of sales negotiations. In practically all cases it is the duty of each side to achieve the very best deal for its respective organization. However, to carry it to the extent of letting the other party lose significantly is about as wise in modern-day business as a "let-the-buyer-beware" attitude by a large retailer. We may win the battle and lose the war. Our reputation can spread. And, if we are dependent upon long-term working relationships, it is wise to strive for win-win outcomes in negotiations. But it is equally important to realize that not all parties with whom we negotiate are as skilled or as aware of negotiating principles as we are. Thus, it is important to be alert for negotiating opponents who are thinking only in terms of the most expeditious way to achieve their own goals, while we are pursuing a cooperative win-win philosophy overall. (See Model for Effective Sales Negotiations on page 8.)

Operations Controller:	"We won't have any equipment available there next week. It will all be on the West Coast."
Sales Rep:	"Oh boy. This request is from North American Tractors. They're one of our top three customers."
Operations Controller:	"Wish I'd known yesterday. We committed three of the big babies to Alpha."
Sales Rep:	"Thank goodness I checked with you. Is there anything we can do?"
Operations Controller:	"Can't think of anything now."
Sales Rep:	"If I could just have one for a couple of days, I think I could talk North American into delaying the rest for a week. Any chance Alpha could let us use one of the three if we have it back to them by next Thursday?"

Rate Yourself

How effective are you at each of the following?

- Recognizing opportunities for give and take.

- Setting high negotiating goals.

- Maintaining tenacity along with flexibility.

- Resisting one-way concessions.

- Preparing well for a negotiation.

- Taking reasonable risks.

- Planning to control the negotiating climate.

- Using effective tactics and counter-tactics.

- Attending to follow-through details.

- Striving for a win-win.

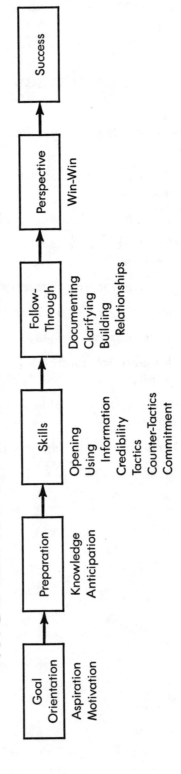

MODEL FOR EFFECTIVE SALES NEGOTIATIONS

Goal Orientation	Preparation	Skills	Follow-Through	Perspective	Success

Goal Orientation
Aspiration
Motivation

Preparation
Knowledge
Anticipation

Skills
Opening
Using Information
Credibility
Tactics
Counter-Tactics
Commitment

Follow-Through
Documenting
Clarifying
Building Relationships

Perspective
Win-Win

Operations Controller:	"I'll try, but I doubt it. They're in a crunch schedule."
Sales Rep:	"Any other tradeoffs you can think of?"
Operations Controller:	"You know, as I recall, Maintenance owes us a favor. They have two of the big ones in for routine scheduling right now. It shouldn't be a big problem for them to release one to us for a couple of days. Yes, I'm sure I can get one from them temporarily."
Sales Rep:	"Great. I really appreciate it—incidentally, find out from maintenance if there is any way I can return the favor."

INTERNAL NEGOTIATIONS FIRST

It is fine to suggest that you do not go into a negotiation before getting agreement in your own organization on the objectives, particularly on the mandatory levels. But oftentimes it is your own people who are most difficult to pin down.

If you find this is the case, it can be useful to step back and put the objectives, as well as the rest of your plan, down in writing. Then, ask your own people to react to that. In other words, you are saying to them, "This is what I intend to do—unless you tell me otherwise."

Let us take the case of Pat Atkins, who has gotten into a bit of an interesting situation with a major customer. Pat has just sold a contract for 32 Z-type conveyor units to Melbourne Services Company, a major provider of cargo transfer services at marine terminals, airports, and warehousing complexes. Pat's company, Transfer Systems, Inc., has just released their new Z line, and management is most anxious to capture as much market share as possible this first year. The Z-type has some clear efficiency advantages over competitors' products, this due to some truly innovative engineering design concepts which should save customers countless man-hours in tight maneuvering situations. Let's check in with Pat and see what's happening.

Wrapping Up a Fantastic Success

There is nothing quite so satisfying to a new sales account executive as that drive back to the office after a very demanding week—a week which has just concluded with the second highest sales contract ever. This was the case with Pat that crisp fall Friday afternoon following the signing of the contract with Melbourne Services. "What a coup! Four months of agonizing negotiations. And frankly, I did very nearly all of it by myself. Fantastic!"

Actually, although it had taken the better part of four months to get Melbourne to a final decision, Pat had encountered only minor resistance to the original proposal of $335,000 for 35 conveyors. That figure had been just a bit over a 4% discount off the list price of $10,000 per conveyor, and, although Melbourne had specified 32 units at the start, Pat had built in a little cushion by pricing out 35.

In the end, Barry Perkins, the assistant purchasing manager at Melbourne, had only been able to get the price down to $9,200 per unit, a fact that Pat was quite proud of. After all, a professional buyer with the skills and experience of a Barry Perkins might reasonably expect to negotiate considerably more than that off a contract proposal of this size.

Of course, there had been all the odds and ends that had been worked out. That was mostly what had required four months to accomplish. It had seemed to take a lot of meetings before Barry had been able to work his way through his own organization's bureaucracy. Over the course of those meetings Pat had agreed to a number of minor points in order to close the final agreement: things like providing an additional safety-catch on the two front wheels; extending the 1%-per-month penalty for payment after 30 days out to 90 days; adding free round-the-clock maintenance for the first 60 days to the standard warranty; and a few lesser details on the delivery schedule and parts stock. Prior to the promotion into the account exec job, Pat had started out in the engineering department at Transfer Systems, and was quite confident that the safety catches involved only minor changes. And considering the size of this contract, the other details had seemed a small price to pay.

Pat's jubilance had been hard to contain when Barry handed over the signed contract early that afternoon. Would Pat's boss, Fran Aikens, ever be pleased with this one! Pat was mildly grateful that Fran had been on vacation those past couple of weeks, and not around to nitpick the contract revisions. Sometimes Pat wondered how Fran had ever become Sales Manager with such a cautious approach to everything. On the other hand it would be good to have Fran back now, to work out all the details with engineering, production, and other departments at Transfer Systems. Sometimes it seemed as though the sales department spent more time coordinating details between customers and internal departments than it did actually selling. "Whatever, that's Fran's problem now with this one."

Now Getting Stomped On

It was late Monday morning before Fran had dug through two weeks of mail and a couple hours of telephone calls. But that had been enough time to figure out some serious concerns over a sales contract Pat Atkins had turned in late Friday afternoon. Pat had apparently committed to deliver 32 of the new Z-type conveyor units to Melbourne Services Company, all within a 30-day time span following the date of the signed contract. That would be difficult, if not impossible. Since the contract was dated last Thursday, that meant only 26 days to go. But the clincher was a late delivery penalty clause to the tune of 1% per week for every conveyor not delivered on time.

At their scheduled mid-morning debriefing, Fran's management skills would be tested. Pat arrived beaming with pride at having sold such a significant order. Fran felt like screaming, "What do you mean you promised 32 Z's by the fifteenth of next month!" But in a considerably less volatile tone Fran managed to compliment Pat for the large order, then diplomatically reviewed "some of the problems we'll need to deal with internally to fulfill our end of the bargain."

The first problem was that two other major customers had placed trial orders during the past week. These orders were not as large as Pat's, but they too were for earliest possible delivery, and depending on those customers' evaluation of the trial orders, there would be significantly more at stake long-term than with Melbourne Services. In both cases the account executives had gone through a bit of give-and-take with the manufacturing scheduling coordinator before making firm commitments to the customers.

Pat pointed out to Fran that there were at least 50 of the new Z's sitting on the lot next to the plant. "They must be cranking them out at the rate of at least five a day to add to that inventory." But what Pat had not realized was that not only were all those 50 some units sold, but that the Z's were actually back-ordered. The reason for the large inventory sitting at the plant was a transportation delay due to a labor dispute in Chicago.

On top of all that, Transfer Systems was having some puzzling problem in manufacturing. Quality control had picked up a defect in the wheel bearings on the new Z units, and all inventory was to be held until that got fixed. It didn't appear to be a major problem, but top management was not about to risk its releasing shipments of a new product line with flaws in it.

"And Pat, I got a call earlier this morning that Melbourne Services has a shaky credit rating. Pat, we're in a bit of a jam here. It seems that everything sneaked up on us while I was away. I guess I should have taken more care to make sure you understood the importance of working all the details of an order of this size through our internal people. There is going to have to be some give-and-take."

While Fran was trying hard not to scold Pat, it was clear that the give-and-take should have occurred before the contract was signed, not after. It was also clear that Pat should have engaged the manufacturing coordinator, the credit manager, and probably the distribution department in that process of give-and-take while negotiating with Melbourne Services. What a way to learn a lesson!

"Well, okay Pat. It's easy enough to say it's water-over-the-dam. But what we have to do now is to figure out how to get out of this pickle. If Melbourne holds us to the fire, somehow both sides are going to have to make some concessions. Here's what we better do—."

Cap in Hand

Next afternoon Pat anxiously waited to be greeted by Barry Perkins outside the conference room at Melbourne Services. It had been a hastily arranged meeting. Barry had probably smelled trouble. Whether it was an act or not, he looked gravely annoyed when Pat tried to explain some "order backlog problems," with a plea either to have the penalty clause removed from the contract, or a revised delivery schedule. Although there had been no cross words in that briefing with Fran the previous day, Pat suspected that the penalty clause was the one thing which had really tested Fran's patience. "What a dumb clause to have agreed to—all in haste—damn!"

"Our people have already gone ahead with a commitment at one of the large marine terminals, Pat. We did that based on the delivery schedule you agreed to. We can't back out of it now or we'll lose a major chunk of business. No way, Pat. You either deliver those conveyors on time or we apply the penalty clause. In fact, if you slip deliveries by too much, and jeopardize our contract with the marine terminal, we'll do a lot more than just exercise a penalty clause."

Barry was tough. He railed on. In fact he threatened to cancel the order if Transfer missed the first scheduled delivery. Pat would have almost preferred that at this point. There was too much at stake: four months of sales effort, a sales commission worth nearly 20% of the entire year's total, and a great deal of credibility all the way through the organization. In the worst possible case, the tone of Barry's veiled threat suggested litigation if Transfer Systems couldn't deliver.

The fact that Pat's initialing of the original contract was probably not legally binding was really a moot issue. If worse came to worse, Pat's lack of authority to sign a contract of this size would not be of much help. The sale would be lost, Melbourne Services would no doubt be lost as a customer for some time to come, and if they decided to get rough about it, costly legal fees could be incurred, regardless of who won the case.

"Incidentally Pat, one of your manufacturing supervisors apparently told one of our maintenance foremen that your people would love to install the safety catch on the front wheels. He said that not only would it not cost your people any significant time and materials but that your own safety and insurance departments had been pressing for the additional catch from the beginning. As I recall, you tacked on an additional $75 per conveyor for that catch. I think if there are any contract revisions, removing that $75 per unit would be the first one."

"Pat, we don't intend to get jerked around. We've got too much at stake on this. I think you'd better get back to your people and get this sorted out. We need that first delivery in just three and a half weeks. We expect to get it."

What a Mess

The following morning back at the office Fran outlined the next step. "Pat, this Melbourne problem has us in a potential pickle with at least two other key customers. I'm calling the other two account execs in for a meeting this afternoon. Smitty, the manufacturing planning supervisor, is joining us. I know Smitty gets emotional, and downright unreasonable at times. But we've got to sit the five of us down in one room and work out a way to satisfy all three customers without causing major convulsions in manufacturing."

Fran paused for a moment, then continued. "Pat, we have a related concern that I'd best let you know about. A few months before you moved into your present job, we were involved in a major dispute

with Melbourne Services over an alleged failure of some of our equipment. You may have heard bits and pieces about this. We were con-
vinced their operators were abusing the equipment. But in the end, to
stay out of a costly legal hassle, Ballinger (vice-president of marketing
at Transfer Systems) worked out a settlement with Melbourne's presi-
dent. They belong to the same club you see, and I think they met over
dinner to keeps things on a semi-amicable basis. The problem now is
that Ballinger is aware of our current predicament and has said in no
uncertain terms that this is to get sorted out without higher level
involvement." Fran's tone of voice left little doubt in Pat's mind as to
the importance of an early solution to the problem.

"Pat, we can try to shove this down manufacturing's throat and tell
them to find a solution. But I can tell you from past experience, we'll
pay a price long term. Smitty has a dozen other balls in the air day-in
and day-out, and frankly that feisty, combative attitude is understand-
able at times. Production scheduling is a hotbed of pressures from all
directions. This afternoon isn't going to be easy.

"Pat, there are a couple of other matters we need to talk about
here. I realize you had to pull a lot of last-minute details together while
I was on vacation. But whether I'm here or not, a lot of the details of a
contract this size need a commitment from our own people first. The
60-day free maintenance is fine. It's part of our strategy. But things
like delivery schedules, modifications, financial terms, and the like
require additional commitments to negotiate these things to a satisfactory level with our own people before we complete the negotiation
with the customer. And as for haggling over the $75 charge for the
additional safety catch, you were right on target for adding that to the
price when Melbourne requested the catch. Then one of our own
supervisors blows it by some dumb statement to his buddy at
Melbourne. There was no way you could have anticipated that. In fact,
maybe I ought to organize some meetings with both the manufacturing and engineering groups so that everyone's on board on these
larger negotiations. It seems that it's always one of our own people
behind-the-scenes who says something to the customer that gives away
half our bargaining powers."

Fran was right. The meeting that afternoon was a toughie. It
wasn't just that Smitty was obstinate. There was genuinely no way
manufacturing was going to be able to meet the demands of all three
customers for the new Z's. The meeting ended in a deadlock with the
ball in Fran's court to make a hard choice as to which customer, and
which account exec, was to be bumped.

Fran's phone rang as the meeting was about to end. "Fran, this is Bernie in the credit department. We've been told we can't extend more than 45 days credit to Melbourne Services due to their poor payment record over the past year..."

Who Blew What?

Regardless of Fran's decision in this case, everybody's life had been made more difficult. Why? You may call it lack of coordination, or poor communication, or even loose management on Fran's part. But the semantics of what we call it doesn't matter much. The fact is in any organization there is a constant balancing act going on. There is a never-ending need for people and departments to negotiate tradeoffs with each other. When those internal tradeoffs are going to impact customers, it is your obligation as the salesperson to be aware of them—and to deal with them.

What had happened to leave both Pat and Fran in such a predicament over Melbourne Services? On the surface the negotiation with Melbourne had gone reasonably well. But Pat had apparently viewed that large order in isolation without thinking about who or what might be impacted within Transfer System's own operation—and caught up in the euphoria of a big order, did not take the time to gain the internal commitments.

Maybe Fran should have anticipated these kinds of problems before going off on vacation. Maybe in the past Fran had not pushed the account executives to do a lot of their own negotiating internally. Maybe Fran had done too much of it for them.

We don't really know what tradeoffs might have been worked out in this case had the manufacturing coordinator been involved earlier. We do know that in most situations there are ample opportunities for some give-and-take if you take time to get the key people involved in the process early-on.

As for the credit department, somebody has now made a policy statement. Whomever that is, they now risk losing credibility if they back down. If they are forced down, they lose face. And they will fight like mad. If Pat or Fran had approached them before the policy decision regarding Melbourne Services' credit restrictions, they might well have worked something out to enhance such a large order. Even had it not been the full credit request, it would have been much easier to negotiate a less lenient credit arrangement with Melbourne before the agreement rather than later. Sure, most companies don't give the sales department that much freedom to negotiate credit terms without prior approval. Transfer Systems did. But whether it is terms of credit or a dozen other negotiable points, you as the salesperson need to be constantly thinking about who in your own organization may be affected. With whom do I need to negotiate this variable in my own organization before I commit to my customer?

So, What Did We Learn?

To answer that, let's briefly look back at the Internal Negotiation's Planner on page 17. Next to each item you need to think about who in your own organization needs to be committed to that item. What problems could a concession on that item create? For whom? Are we willing to concede anything on that item? If so, how much? The only way to answer these questions is to do some internal negotiating first. The negotiating plan is not in order until you have satisfied yourself that those people in your own manufacturing department, customer service department, credit department, technical department, etc., are able and willing to fulfill the commitments you are making to the customer. This is not to suggest that you check every minor point with them. But on major points where tradeoffs may be necessary, you will save yourself, and others, untold conflict downstream if you take the time for a little internal give-and-take.

INTERNAL NEGOTIATIONS PLANNER

Internal People I Should Negotiate with on This sale	Issues to Be Negotiated	My Objectives	Their Objectives & Concerns	Tradeoffs & Compromise Possibilities	Outcome

Rate Yourself on Your Internal Negotiating

How effective are you at working out the internal give-and-take in your own organization before you commit to the buyer?

- Taking time to negotiate with your own internal people.

- Anticipating those items in a sales agreement which need some internal negotiating.

- Checking your assumptions regarding your ability to deliver all aspects of the sales agreement.

- Managing your own enthusiasm in a productive way.

- Developing healthy relationships with those internal people you may need to negotiate with.

- Staying on top of those things operating in your own organization which may affect your customers.

- Keeping your boss well-informed of major sales agreements as they are developing.

- Anticipating the kinds of information your own internal people should keep to themselves.

- Checking out your customer's history in terms of how it may affect a current internal negotiation.

- Getting both customers and internal people to actively seek alternatives when internal roadblocks occur.

- Sensing those issues in a sales agreement which could pose internal credibility and face-saving problems.
- Planning your internal negotiating needs.

2

ESTABLISHING OBJECTIVES AND TARGETS

Sales Manager:	"Have you thought through how you are going to deal with Itex Manufacturing tomorrow?"
Sales Rep:	"I sure have. I'll be asking $4,000 a unit."
Sales Manager:	"They'll scream about that, won't they?"
Sales Rep:	"Yes, but Service and Engineering have helped me put together plenty of justification."
Sales Manager:	"I'm glad you got them involved, but what if Itex resists?"
Sales Rep:	"There are a couple of tradeoffs I can offer them on the specifications, which I have found they want very badly."
Sales Manager:	"How much will the tradeoffs cost us?"
Sales Rep:	"Almost nothing. But I'm not offering them unless Itex concedes on price."
Sales Manager:	"Good. Sounds like you are ready."
Sales Rep:	"I think so. I've laid it all out on this worksheet. Could I talk it through with you now, just to get your final input?"
Sales Manager:	"Let's do it."

ESTABLISHING OBJECTIVES AND TARGETS

The first step in most successful sales negotiations is effective planning. In fact lack of effective planning is probably a bigger cause of losing in negotiations than any weakness in the execution of the face-to-face bargaining process.

The first step in the planning process is to establish your objectives or targets for the final outcome expected in the negotiation. As the saying goes, "If you don't know where you are going, any road will take you there." It is sometimes tempting to quickly set a target, almost from "gut feel" of the situation, and to move unhesitatingly into the fun part of the conjuring up of various strategies and tactics we expect to employ against our opponents. The setting of objectives and targets should not be taken that lightly. There are oftentimes changing factors which need to be considered before we lock into a mind-set based on our past experience and related assumptions.

In any given negotiations there may be a number of objectives to be considered and balanced against each other. It may not be sufficient simply to say, "my target is to sell this contract for $40,000, period." There may be several tradeoffs we need to consider. Finding the best mix of objectives and tradeoffs is what sales negotiation is all about.

The Widget Example

In securing a contract for 1,000 widgets, our primary objective may be to confirm a selling price of $10,000. We may also need to secure the order prior to the end of the month (and would be willing to bend a bit on the price to achieve this). "To finalize the contract before the end of the month" then is an additional objective. This could leave us with two pricing objectives: $10,000 is now our high target objective while $9,500 may be our minimum acceptable price objective. Some objectives may be absolute or mandatory—e.g., $9,500—whereas, others may be negotiable—e.g., $10,000. The point is we need to have established a high but realistic target in advance and then have determined exactly how far we are willing to negotiate; e.g., the absolute or mandatory level. Now if we carry this example a bit further, we could list any number of other objectives regarding the contract which may be negotiable. Quality of the materials, surface finish, delivery times, credit terms, and any number of other things may be taken for granted because of our normal way of doing business. But we might easily use these as negotiable items, especially if bending a little could make life easier for one party without any sacrifice by the other.

It is a balanced outcome that the salesperson and the buyer need to look for. It is quite possible that some of the buyer's objectives are not in conflict with yours, and that preparing to concede a little in one area will make it easier for the buyer to bend some in another. These factors all need to be thought through during the target and objective setting stage of negotiations planning.

Raising Your Expectation Levels

Salespeople with high but realistic targets generally fare better in negotiations than those with more modest targets. That may sound simple enough, but the crux of the issue is, "How much are you willing to risk?" or "How high is high?" It is no problem to set a high target. But, are you willing, for example, to stick to your $10,000 price for widgets right down to the end of the month, risking loss of the contract. Certainly, if you are willing to settle for $9,500, the higher above that you set your original sights the more apt you are to arrive at a final price above $9,500 (provided the buyer doesn't scrap the whole negotiation because he thinks you're not realistic).

Taking Reasonable Risks

Research studies at Harvard University have shown that "higher achievers" place a high value on their own productivity, that they are hard workers, and that they are generally optimistic about the impact they will have on the results. The research has further shown that high achievers tend to take *reasonable risks*—that is, they do not opt for a sure thing, since that offers little challenge, and they avoid high risk situations. Furthermore, they are patient, but want to be kept abreast of their progress. And, they are better planners than modest achievers are, particularly in the long range. In essence, this research has indicated that high achievers set high goals, they expect to reach those goals, and they do achieve those goals more frequently than people with modest aspirations and with minimal willingness to take risk.

One of the things that gets in the way of setting high targets and taking reasonable risks is failure. It seems that every time a salesperson gets burned and loses a negotiation, he's inclined to be gun-shy next time around, take a little less risk, and set a slightly lower target. Conversely, a success fosters the opposite reaction; i.e., willingness to take a greater risk and the setting of higher targets.

Studies at the University of Southern California showed a direct correlation between negotiators with high aspiration levels making high opening demands, or offers, and the level of success in the outcomes of the negotiations. In those studies clearly negotiators with relatively low opening demands or offers fared poorly in the final results. Other research studies have confirmed these findings and have further indicated that this direct correlation holds true up to the point where the negotiator loses credibility due to unrealistically high demands (or low offers), whereupon deadlock in the negotiation usually results.

If as the sales negotiator you have done your homework to the point that you know roughly the point at which your opening demand would appear unrealistic to the prospective buyer, then set your targets just below that, you are at your optimum opening bargaining position. And, of course, price alone is not the sole factor in that opening demand—additional services, credit extension, assurances of reliability, and all other potential benefits which can be negotiated should have targets and mandatory levels fixed on them before the live bargaining begins.

Avoiding Too Much Logic and Reasonableness

One of the pitfalls in trying to establish or maintain a long term relationship with a buyer, particularly with inexperienced negotiators, is the desire to establish an image of "rational and reasonable." There is nothing wrong with being rational and reasonable, but the difficulty is that it's so often based on untested assumptions. What the salesperson thinks is reasonable, based on assumptions (maybe based on what was reasonable in the past), could be extremely generous to the buyer, especially if conditions or circumstances have changed recently.

Take, for example, Pan State Contractors who had a large construction contract delayed due to equipment failure. They were nearing a deadline, and if they missed it, it would cost them thousands of dollars in contract penalties. In dire need of replacement equipment, they called the sales rep in from Reliable Equipment Supplies to arrange an urgent delivery. The sales rep, anxious to break into this new account, granted better than usual discounts, generous credit terms, and absorbed air freight charges to get the equipment delivered quickly—all to the tune of reducing a normal net profit of 20% to just below 5%. And he conceded all this simply because Pan State Contractors requested it—no counter-offers, no negotiating, and no testing of assumptions.

Logic told this sales rep that if he were "reasonable" with this new account in need he would gain future business. He did. But he would have anyway, he learned later, for Pan State Contractors had already decided to give their future business to Reliable Equipment. The sales rep's targets were too loose and too vulnerable without some rigorous testing of his assumptions about the buyer's intentions.

Fix Those Targets High!

In fact, first of all, fix some targets. If there is a list price, don't assume that nobody will pay it until they tell you they won't.

One requirement of effective negotiating is sufficient elbow room. Room to negotiate implies the need for as wide a margin as is realistic between that mandatory level, below which you can't go, and your initial opening demand. In sales negotiations set your sights high, establish a high set of initial targets, and support those targets with enough rationale to maintain credibility. Do these things and you will come out best in the long run.

Of course, it is always useful to have some fix on the other person's targets before the negotiating begins. The wider the gap between his goals and your own suggests the need to do as much preliminary research as possible; *one,* to counter his offer if it is not in line with the facts and *two,* to support your own demands. Turn the tables for a moment. When a car salesman quotes you a $12,000 price on a new car, how do you know what a reasonable counter-offer would be. You do some research. You check the published paperbacks in the bookstore to see how much the dealer actually paid for the car. Then you compare with others who have recently bought a similar car. You may read trade literature and consumer periodicals to find out what current prices are. A little time involved in research can go a long way in letting you know what the other party's real mandatory targets are and what your own high targets should be.

Seven Principles of Establishing Objectives and Targets

- Discipline yourself not to begin negotiating without a clear idea as to what your targets and objectives are, or what information you need in order to establish them.
- Set high targets, allowing plenty of elbow room should you find it necessary to make concessions.
- Do your homework. Be sure you can justify your rationale for each objective or target to the extent that the buyer will perceive it as realistic, even though it is high.

- Develop a worksheet or checklist for negotiations objective setting, particularly for larger, more complex negotiations.
- For team negotiations get the input from each team member, then obtain a firm commitment from each to support the objectives and targets you have set.
- Prepare to negotiate as vigorously within your own team and organization, to establish high targets, as you will with the buyer organization in the actual negotiations.
- Check your targets and objectives for each negotiation with your management to verify the acceptable mandatory levels and to gain support for your negotiating range(s).

Involving the Right People

In doing your homework for a negotiation plan, it is useful to make a list of everybody who may be able to provide useful information regarding each aspect of the negotation plan. In establishing the objectives, a salesperson is wise to get input from all sources who could reasonably contribute: market research people, production, finance, and other internal groups as well as sources outside the organization. Target setting is not an off-the-top-of-the-head process.

Many different departments, plans, people, and egos can be affected by a sales negotiation. Any one of these has the potential to throw a monkey-wrench into the fulfillment of a bargaining agreement if their concerns and interests are adversely affected by the final outcome. Therefore, it is always wise to seek input from those people and groups who will be significantly affected by any negotiated terms of an agreement.

Planning the Role of the Salesperson

In team negotiations, each member of the team has a different set of expertise to contribute. Ordinarily, nobody on the team has the contacts, the access and the overall knowledge of the buyer organization (with whom you are negotiating) as the salesperson responsible for that account. It is the salesperson then, who can provide the strategic information and the market intelligence about the organization with whom the bargaining is to take place.

Although the technical and accounting people on the team can provide the basic information to establish the mandatory or required minimum negotiating objectives, it is the salesperson who understands the psychology and interrelationships within the buyer organization, who can offer the greatest insights into fixing the high targets and the opening demands which will raise the net profits to maximum potential. It is indeed the salesperson's responsibility to have learned enough about the interworkings of the buyers to be prepared to make that contribution.

Key Elements of Negotiation Objectives

In establishing the objectives, it is necessary to consider *minimum requirements* (we must get a minimum of 9 cents a pound), *constraints* (the maximum we can produce are 3,000 units per month), *optimum levels* (2,000 of Item A and 1,000 of Item B would give us the most efficient mix), and *other desirable outcomes* (we would like to do this with our present work force). To list all the meaningful objectives in each of these four areas it is useful to use the five W's and the H:

WHO	can contribute to and who will be affected by this negotiation?
WHAT	is the maximum and minimum (mandatory and high) targets we will seek?
WHEN	*must* we conclude this negotiation and when would we *like to* conclude?
WHERE	is the best place for us to negotiate?
WHY	has the buyer selected us to negotiate with—does this suggest any bargaining strengths for our side?
HOW	willing are we to make concessions and how will we seek counter-concessions from the other party?

Negotiable Items to Be Included

There are unlimited numbers of items that could be listed as factors to be considered for setting targets and objectives for any given negotiation. However, most factors can generally be derived from one of these six categories:

1. Quality– any failure within 10,000 hours of usage will be corrected free of charge.
2. Quantity– they must commit to purchase at least $25,000 worth per month—or, they must commit to at least 50% of our expanded output—or, we can guarantee them ten blue if they will take five red per delivery.
3. Timing– We could make a price concession if they will take half in March and the other half in May.

4. Related & Supplementary– could we tie the contract renewal in California to this one in New York—or, we could make a price concession on widgets if they will renegotiate the contract on pumps—or, we could bend a little on the heavy machines if they could include us as a secondary source on their supplies—or, we have an inventory of spare parts which we would like to include in this contract.

5. Bargaining Strengths– our price is firm since none of our competitors can meet their delivery schedule requirements—or, for some reason they are unhappy with their present vendor, maybe because of poor service, or maybe because of pressure to cancel some other contracts.

6. Pricing/Value– they can definitely cut out one step in their production process if they use our material, which outweighs the additional 2 cents per pound.

Devise an Objective Setting Worksheet

To summarize all the thinking and inputs into the setting of objectives and target levels, it is helpful to assemble the vital information on a worksheet. (See Sample Sales Negotiations Objectives Setting Worksheet on page 29.) The objectives worksheet then becomes the launching pad for planning the negotiation.

You may wish to tailor-design worksheets appropriate to each negotiation. Certain key elements need to be considered whatever format is used. The pricing objectives as well as important quality, quantity, timing, and other related issues need to be considered. Opening demands (high target) and negotiating limits (mandatory levels) should be considered for each objective. Estimate the buyer's targets. Note which people or departments are to be considered. List the bargaining strengths and approvals, as well as other inputs and minor issues, to be considered. Use this format, revise and redesign this format, but use some format. There is nothing more useful in planning, and particularly in that first step of objective and target setting, than to record the important information on a visible and well-organized chart.

Do Some Internal Negotiating

Since many different people and groups may be involved in preparing for a negotiation, some differences in opinion and perception of the issues is inevitable. Therefore, the wise and weathered sales

SAMPLE SALES NEGOTIATIONS OBJECTIVES SETTING WORKSHEET

OBJECTIVE	HIGH TARGET LEVEL (Opening Level)	MANDATORY LEVEL (Won't go below)	BUYER'S TARGET ESTIMATED	WHO INPUTS OR IS AFFECTED	BARGAINING STRENGTHS	APPROVED PRIORITY
Pricing/Value				Production Cost Accounting Credit & Collections	Buyer has indicated a pressing need due to a new contract they have landed.	High Medium
• price per unit	$36	$27	$26			
• terms	2% net 30	2% net 90	2% net 90			
Quality				Customer Service Production Control		Medium High
• warranty	One year	Two years	30 months			
• specification	97.5%	99%	99.5%			
Quantity				Production Distribution		Medium Low
• per delivery	144	100	100			
• mix	half red	2 to 1	2 to 1			
Timing				Production Distribution Customer Service	Buyer has implied delivery problems with Competitor X	High
• delivery schedule	Wed./Thurs.	Not before Wed.	Wed./Thurs.			
• first delivery	June 10	Not before June 3	Soon as possible			Medium
Related Issues				Customer Service		Medium
• service contract	$5 K per year	no contract	no contract			
• renegotiate specs	6 months	- - - - -	no			High

Other Items: Buyer may wish one day free process training for personnel (OK if requested).

negotiator expects to have to conduct some effective negotiating within his or her own organization before a solid negotiation plan can be finalized.

Sales Rep:	"Let's offer to modify the mobile apparatus so they will need to use our service add-on."
Cost Accountant:	"We can't do that because of the inevitable cost overruns."
Engineer:	"Maybe we should do a make-or-buy analysis on that."
Production Manager:	"If you would let us cut out the auxiliary pump, we could do it within costs anyway."
Legal Department:	"You'd have to secure an amendment to the contract before considering that."

And so it goes. Internal negotiation is a very critical part of many sales negotiations. Time must be allotted for it and it should occur before you get caught short with your back to the wall in the "for keeps" bargaining with the buyer or customer.

The very first thing that needs to be negotiated internally are the objectives, especially the mandatory levels. As the sales negotiator, you can set as high a target as your judgment of the buyer's perception of realism will permit. But unless all key internal parties are committed to the "very worst" agreement you could come out with, the follow-through troubles can be endless. If the credit manager is upset over the terms you have negotiated, much abrasion can occur over the life of the contract. If the engineering department thinks you have conceded too much on design, front end delays can become interminable. If distribution thinks you have bowed to unrealistic delivery schedules, better go buy some Mylanta. Your troubles can be endless if you fail to negotiate acceptable internal commitments.

Objectives and targets are your first step in the negotiation process. The better you have thought them through and firmed them up, the smoother the sailing ahead.

Rate Yourself as a Planner

How effective are you at each of the following in planning to negotiate with a buyer? (See also Negotiation's Objectives Setting Worksheets on pages 29 and 32.)

- Taking time to plan.
- Thinking through the possible tradeoffs.
- Pushing your targeted demands as high as possible.
- Preparing "reasons" to explain these demands to the buyer.
- Identifying easy, but useful, concessions to make.
- Recognizing and testing your assumptions.
- Identifying all your objectives.
- Getting a fix on the buyer's objectives in advance.
- Using some sort of checklist in advance.
- Involving others in your planning.
- Answering who, what, when, where, why, and how.
- Identifying issues in quality, quantity, timing, related business, bargaining strengths, and value pricing.
- Knowing both your mandatory level and highest expectation on each key target.
- Using a worksheet to plan.
- Identifying internal people with vested interests in this negotiation.
- Getting internal commitments in your own organization.

NEGOTIATIONS OBJECTIVES SETTING WORKSHEET

Objective	High Target (Opening Level)	Mandatory Level (Won't Go Below)	Buyer's Target (Your Estimate)	Who Inputs or Is Affected	Bargaining Strengths	Approved Priority
Pricing/Value						
Quality						
Quantity						
Timing						
Related Issues						
Other Items						

3

HOW TO TAP
IMPORTANT SOURCES
OF INFORMATION

Sales Rep:	"Sam, could you find out from one of your engineering friends at Itex what they are really looking for in terms of specifications, as well as something about their maintenance and servicing problems?"
Sam: (Engineering Manager)	"I'm pretty sure I can. I'll get back to you tomorrow."
Sales Rep:	"Great. Be careful not to mention to them our projected cost savings on your new design features."
Sam:	"Right. I understand."

(Now in conversation with boss.)

Sales Rep:	"Sam is getting some key information for us from some of his counterparts at Itex."
Sales Manager:	"Good. Is there anybody else who can help us put the total picture together for this negotiation?"
Sales Rep:	"I think so. Here is an information-gathering checklist I've put together with names of people both here and at Itex I intend to contact. Take a look at it."

Sales Manager: "Looks good. I see you have me down for cost details. Let's meet tomorrow morning and go through that."

OUTLINING INFORMATION NEEDS

Once the objectives and target levels are set, approved, and prioritized, the next step in the planning process is to determine what information will be needed. Some information must be gathered in advance and other information will not come out until you are meeting face-to-face. The more thorough job you do in gathering advance information, the more effective your strategies and tactics will be.

Information is the foundation of bargaining strength. In determining what kinds of information you will need, a first step is to make a laundry list of everything that seems important regarding each of the objectives you have listed. A second, and most vital, step is to then list all the *assumptions* you and your boss, or other support people, are making (e.g., Competitor B is offering the usual terms), and what information you need in order to test these assumptions.

Tapping Sources of Information

Internal sources include all the people and departments within your organization you have identified in the objective setting process as well as other people within the sales function who are familiar with competitors, with similar buyers and with new developments in the marketplace. Higher management frequently has access to additional information. They should be made aware of any critical information you need and with which you are having difficulty.

One of the primary external sources of information are the people within the organization with whom you will be negotiating. As the sales rep or account executive, you may well have access to technical people, shipping and receiving personnel, service people, and other employees of your account. They can be valuable sources of "informal" information regarding competitor activity, new developments, and marketing plans—any kind of information which may give you a fix on the targets and strategies you will be facing in the negotiation. A list of these potential sources, both internal and external, including other companies and organizations, is a vital tool in beginning your information-gathering effort.

Assembling Product and Service Information

Charlie Sellers leases private aircraft to corporations for executive transportation. In casually chatting with the maintenance supervisor at the hangar one day, he learned that the executives of a major customer had voiced a strong opinion that their company should switch to a different leasing organization at contract renewal time due to more "comfortable" interiors in the aircraft of the competitor firm.

Charlie asked the maintenance person to get a few more details first chance he could. This proved to be an invaluable information source as Charlie found that with just a few moderate cost modifications he was able to satisfy the wants of these executives, more than pay for the expenses in the new lease agreement, and gain a permanent, useful source of "market intelligence" in the maintenance supervisor (who was appropriately rewarded).

There are seven key areas of product and service information that a sales negotiator needs to consider:

1. *Product/Service Specifications.* Technical and legal constraints, individual preferences, and meshing with marketing plans and other systems.
2. *Maintenance and Servicing.* Customers' capabilities and strategies; your own vs. competitors; tie in with similar requirements on other products and services.
3. *Design Constraints.* Lead times, make-or-buy decisions, subcontracts, and long term plans.
4. *Production or Operations.* Modifications required, timing, mix, union contracts, growth, skills, and equipment.
5. *Tradeoffs.* Any product or service variables.
6. *Packaging and Distribution.* Transport mode, related packing required, quantity savings, and timing.
7. *Marketplace.* Trends, developments, and competitive practices.

After listing each item of information needed in each category, compare it to your objectives worksheet, testing both sheets for new inputs and thoroughness. It is then useful to place priorities on each of these information items in order to invest your limited time resources in that research which offers the greatest potential payoff.

Getting Cost, Pricing and Budget Information

The following five areas of costing, pricing, and budgeting information can seem like an endless flow of data, like a bowl full of jelly, or like something that only the financial freaks understand (and manipulate):

- Direct Costs—historical, current or replacement cost depreciation methods?
- Indirect Costs—based on what assumptions?
- Budget Timing—are budgets negotiable?
- Pricing—affected by Robinson-Patman or other legal or contractual constraints?
- Value Analysis—what's it really worth to the buyer?

Bargaining parameters on both sides of a negotiation can be affected by almost mystical, certainly exotic, cost accounting practices. Concepts such as escalator clauses, inflation factors, allocation methods, and the like must be clearly understood by the sales negotiator in many situations where homework becomes most crucial before wading into the thick of the live negotiation.

Beware of the bargaining opponent who marches into a negotiation with reams and reams of cost data and financial statistics. First of all, that sort of approach can be a tactic or a ploy to divert your attention away from the buyer's bargaining weaknesses. Secondly, it may introduce an unrealistic element into the bargaining in terms of time and manpower available to test the validity and assumptions used in assembling the data. Thirdly, it could be that the negotiator who does this sort of thing simply does not understand the negotiating process. And finally, much of the data could be misleading or irrelevant to the extent that it is invalid in the particular negotiation and requires a cost accountant or analyst to dissect it and disprove its application.

The point of all this is to emphasize the importance of preparing adequately to deal with the *relevant* financial aspects of a planned negotiation. If it's appropriate, plan a briefing session with the cost experts in your organization. Get them to describe to you what the direct costs are, what the major indirect cost issues are, and what key assumptions have been made in assigning these costs. The analysts may also be able to help you think through the kinds of cost issues your buyer might introduce into the negotiation, both valid and invalid.

It is always useful to dry-run critical segments of a negotiation in advance with the various information sources in your organization. The financial people may well be able to assume the role of your negotiating buyer in a mock situation and test your understanding and methods of dealing with sticky cost issues before you have to confront them "live."

To put this back into a win-win perspective, there can be many opportunities in a negotiation to help the other side find better solutions if you are well-drilled, not only in your own cost analysis, but in anticipating some of the issues your buyer needs to deal with on his side of the table. It is the true professional who can suggest win-win tradeoffs that help both sides. "If you will accept delivery prior to December 31, we can give you a 2% discount (and reduce our own inventory costs by 6%)." "We can reduce your interest costs by as much as $12,000 if you will let us delay delivery of the subcomponents by 90 days (and let us take advantage of some new technology which won't be available for another two months, significantly reducing our production cost)."

Aside from doing some cost analysis, it is important to step back and ask, "What is this product or this service really *worth* to the buyer." After all, he may need your product so badly that he is willing to pay you a 20% surcharge just to speed up delivery by a week.

If he is, forget about the logical asking price, plan to give him an opening demand of 30% surcharge, and don't feel guilty about taking 25. For if he accepts, you are probably both in a win-win outcome.

Gathering Information About the Other Organization

One way of viewing the organization with whom you will be negotiating is in terms of the decision they must make as a result of the negotiation. You need to gather information about their past negotiating practices, strategies, and tactics, as well as the strengths and characteristics of their negotiators. But you also need to understand specifically what they are trying to accomplish in this negotiating decision:

1. How does this negotiation fit into *their overall* marketing or production *plans?*
2. What are *their* mandatory *objectives* and *targets?*
3. What *secondary benefits* would *they* like to achieve?

4. What other *alternatives* do *they* have that we are competing with?

5. How do *we* compare to those *other alternatives*?

6. What *difficulties or risks* might *they* realize by selecting us, or by selecting *another* alternative?

To answer these questions it is necessary to get inside their organization. Establish channels with as many of their people and departments as you can—technical people, salespeople, marketing, customer service, production—anybody who might give you clues as to what kind of a decision they need to make and why. This suggests the need to begin paving the way many months before a major negotiation is to begin; asking well-planned questions and recording both facts and attitudes.

Let's analyze a bit more each of the six decision-making questions mentioned above.

1. *Their Overall Plans*—This can be difficult to gain information about unless you have a close working relationship with them, or with some other source who knows a great deal about them. It can be extremely useful though, to access in advance how well your proposal is going to fit into their broader marketing and production or service plans.

2. *Their Objectives and Targets*—Already discussed, but in the framework of their decision-making process it is the next step and is directly related to overall plans. Determine how costly their major targets will be to your organization. If you can prepare to make concessions (slowly) on the one's which are not too costly to you, you can then use these to ask for important concessions in return.

3. *Secondary Benefits They Want*—Plan to use these as concession items if they aren't going to cost you much. Plan to resist the costly ones. If they are secondary you aren't risking that much by resisting.

4. *Their Other Alternatives*—You need to find out what they are. Are they deciding on a make-or-buy? Which competitors are in the range of possibility? Is some combination a possibility—if so, how would you best fit in? Is a decision not to buy at all a possibility?

5. *How Do We Compare*—With the other alternatives, in terms of steps 1, 2, and 3 above, and step 6 below. What additional information can we reasonably gather in this area?

6. *Their Difficulties and Risks*—If they go with us? If they select some other alternative? Can we minimize risks and difficulties our proposal might cause? Can we use risks and difficulties posed by other alternatives as bargaining strengths?

Protecting Information

Remember, the other guys would like to find out the same kinds of information about you. Certain types of information must be kept in confidence—like bargaining weaknesses (e.g., we must sell this contract, even at break-even; or, our direct costs are much lower than the buyer realizes; or, we are faced with a possible labor walkout next month). In protecting this type of sensitive information it is desirable to make your internal people aware of the hazards of information leaks, especially during informal discussions with friends, family, and business acquaintances.

Study the information grid on page 40 and think about how it might help you to analyze an upcoming negotiation.

Information Needs Checklist

Product/service specifications.

Maintenance and servicing factors.

Design constraints.

Production or operations factors.

Tradeoffs.

Packaging and distribution factors.

Marketplace factors.

The buyer's overall marketing or production plans.

Their mandatory objectives and targets.

The secondary benefits they want.

Their other alternatives.

Our strength vs. the alternatives.

The buyer's risks.

Buyer: "Look, I've got to go to a meeting in ten minutes. I need a 15% discount. Can you do it or not?"

Seller: "That's quite a bit, Terry, especially when our costs have just gone up."

Buyer: "Time is short. Can you give me 15% or not?"

Seller: "Terry, since we're both under some time pressure, can we do this one on the current pricing, then try to work something out on the next one?"

USING AN
INFORMATION GRID

Enter key information in the appropriate spaces regarding the organization you will be negotiating with in terms of *their* decision-making process in this negotiation.

Role of this Negotiation, in overall marketing/production/service plans:				They need this raw material to launch their new product line. No other raw material is feasible.	
OBJECTIVES & TARGETS	IMPORTANCE	ALTERNATIVE A (Your Proposal)	ALTERNATIVE B (Prime Competitor)	ALTERNATIVE C (Produce In-House)	ALTERNATIVE D (Go Without)
Contract Price $75,000	Mandatory Maximum	Our minimum is $72,500	Probable minimum 65 - $70,000	Take at least 12 months longer	Not feasible
Need 7,000 lbs. per/mo.	High	Can Do	Doubtful	Yes, after 12 mos. delay	Not Feasible
1-year contract	Low	Want 3-year	Probably want 2-to 3-year	Not Applicable	Not Applicable
Difficulties and Risks with each alternative ⬆		Minimal	Cannot produce fast enough Poor reliability in past	Requires $500,000 capital investment	Lose long-range market position

INFORMATION GRID

Role of this negotiation, in Buyer's overall
marketing/production/service plans:

	Importance	Alternative A (your proposal)	Alternative B ( )	Alternative C ( )	Alternative D ( )
Objectives & Targets					
Difficulties and Risks with each alternative					

Rate Yourself as an Information Gatherer

How effective are you at gathering information which will be useful in a negotiation? (See also Information Grid on page 41.)

- Getting your own support people to gather information for you.

- Getting to people inside the buyer organization for information.

- Contacting third parties for information about the buyer.

- Thoroughly understanding your own product/service tradeoff possibilities.

- Gathering cost and pricing information.

- Getting a feel for the real value this may be to the buyer.

- Finding out the buyer's probable objectives, alternatives, and risks.

- Understanding the buyer's decision-making process in advance.

- Protecting critical information which should not be leaked.

- Organizing an information-gathering checklist or grid.

Buyer	"You're being unreasonable. There is no reason you can't give me a 15% break."
Seller·	"Terry, I'd like to work something out. But we need more time to work it through. I can't do it just off the top of my head."
Buyer:	"It's not that complicated."
Seller:	"Terry, you're ordering 20. I can give you 5% if you'll order 50; 10 if you'll take a 100."
Buyer:	"Look, I gotta go. Is that the best you can do?"
Seller:	"Yes, for right now. But I'm sure that next order we can work something out if we have a little more lead time."
Buyer:	"Okay, okay. I'll take 50 at 5%. But I expect 10% retroactive on the next 50."
Seller:	"Thanks, Terry. We'll work something out."

ANTICIPATING DISCIPLINE FACTORS

The best laid plans of mice and negotiators can go awry, at least in the case of the negotiator, if he fails to adhere to the disciplines necessary to avert the myriad of pressures that can send one off course. Have you ever seen a person who is an excellent planner, but who can never seem to execute effectively simply because he cannot resist being diverted by every little shift that comes along. Remember, the other side has a plan too, and if they are skilled, they are going to try many, many ploys to move you into concert with their plan rather than with yours.

The problem with negotiating is that by definition it includes a measure of discretion on the part of the negotiator. Your buyer's goal, especially in a win-lose, is to persuade you, or to pressure you into using your discretion, to grant them the best deal possible. And pressure is a very effective way of doing that. The difficulty for the sales negotiator is that so often you feel almost a compulsion to get that contract, or to confirm the order, that you almost automatically sense that the customer or potential buyer holds all the trump cards. This is a dangerous, and frequently invalid assumption. The purchasing people across the table from you are often under as much pressure as you are, but are more attuned to the art of negotiating, and conceal the pressure they are bearing.

It is useful to spend a little time anticipating some of the things that are likely to go wrong in a negotiation, and to tighten up your discipline in planning to deal with such pitfalls. To protect those well-conceived plans, strategies, and tactics let us take a look at some "do nots."

Avoiding Pitfalls to Effective Negotiation

There are limitless threats to the effective execution of a negotiating plan. Four most common areas of concern are:

- The temptation to rush it.
- Failure to protect, to gather, and to use information.
- Making unnecessary concessions.
- Letting your ego interfere.

1. *The Temptation to Rush-It*—If in the planning steps some sort of *time line* has been plotted to give a visual fix on the pacing strategies, and if deadlock tactics have been thought through, and if all other time related tactics have been considered, there should be no need to negotiate in careless haste. Yet it happens all the time. Why?

First of all we just can't wait to seal the deal, to taste success, to make that kill. After all, as sales types we gotta make things happen. Right, as long as what we make happen is to our side's advantage; and to the other side's if possible.

Example: one of the big warehouses had a severe temperature problem. Everything in it got too hot and is now below spec. Gotta sell it, get rid of it—fast. Now stop a minute—hold it, hold it! There's 100,000 pounds of that stuff. Do you know what an extra 3 cents a pound is worth?

Not only do sales negotiators often tend to rush, giving away $3,000 here—$5,000 there—but we also let the other side rush us. It could be a ploy on their part to get a commitment before we recognize their bargaining weaknesses, or it could be a genuine need to wrap up an agreement. Whatever the reason, a pinch of patience can be worth a pound of hindsight, or something like that. There is no more classic illustration of haste making waste than in negotiations, and no more classic demand for self-discipline to avoid the costly errors that result.

If you are confident the buyer is acting in good faith, and is in genuine need of an early commitment it may even be better to grant the immediate commitment with an understanding that certain items will be negotiated later. This is not always appropriate but consider it as one option with trusted customers. If worse comes to worse, you can always plead no authority, get a sudden tummy-ache, or ask to make a quick phone call. But whatever happens, buy some time to think and to avoid a damaging hurry-up decision.

Another rush-type situation an inexperienced negotiator is apt to fall prey to is caused by talking too much and pausing to listen too little. This seems to be a very tough discipline to learn, especially when up against an experienced buyer who is skilled at pausing and listening. As soon as he pauses the seller feels the need to fill that silence with words, to hasten along the negotiating process. Oh, if we could only discipline ourselves to be patient and to listen; how much useful information we might gain and how much we might avoid giving away—which leads us to a second pitfall area.

2. *Failure to Protect, to Gather, and to Use Information*
The major disciplines to keep in mind here are:

- Do not give away information you don't have to.

- Begin a disciplined gathering of information allowing plenty of lead time prior to the negotiation.

- Use information gathered during the live bargaining to modify your negotiating plan.

- Maintain a disciplined record of information gathered both prior to and during the negotiation.

If you tell a prospective buyer that your technical people have achieved some significant cost savings, his expectations will be raised and he will push that much harder for you to lower your asking price. If you, or anybody else in your organization, lets slip that you need to sell off a facility or some product as soon as possible in order to raise cash for some other needs, then your potential buyers may push you to the hilt for concessions, because they know you have a time deadline to meet.

In fact, anytime you have any of your technical or financial or support people in a meeting with a customer, talk through in advance what kinds of nuggets of information not to give away during the discussions. Some information you need to share, especially in a win-win climate, but discipline yourself and your team not to give away more than is necessary to achieve your negotiation objectives.

On the other hand, if you know that you will be in a negotiation in the foreseeable future, discipline yourself and your team to begin a systematic process of gathering, and sharing with each other, information about the other organization. Do this three months, six months, or even a year in advance. Without a disciplined approach to this information gathering it is so easy to get caught up in day-to-day pressures. Then, suddenly, a negotiation is upon you and you are ill-prepared to deal with a skilled buyer. When this happens you are suddenly thrust back into the first pitfall, a rushed and dangerously hasty negotiation. These disciplines all fit together and will either reinforce or detract from each other.

As in any other effort, the investment of front-end-time can offer considerable payoff in the long term. But it seems to require so much discipline to force oneself to make that investment. Why scouting has been such an integral part of sports for so long and such a slip-shod process in sales negotiations is difficult to answer, especially considering the pride which modern industry takes in scientific business approaches. We can figure out how to gather information in advance, but so often we simply don't do it.

On the other end of the spectrum are those negotiators who do a good job in gathering advance data and in planning, but who somehow get so locked into their plan that they refuse to modify it once new information is introduced during the bargaining. This is as sinful as not gathering information in advance.

A sales negotiator must be flexible enough to change a target or a strategy, as soon as it becomes clearly appropriate from the nature of the bargaining discussion. But the discipline to be followed is to test the validity of that new information before it leads to shaky and damaging assumptions.

Test it by probing, by questioning, and by listening.

The final area of disciplines related to the gathering and using of information is that of recording it. So many unnecessary misunderstandings, incorrect assumptions, and internal dissensions within a negotiating team occur simply because nobody bothered to record what was actually said or seen or heard. Good recordkeeping is as important a discipline in preparing for a negotiation as in any other aspect of business activity. Discipline yourself and your team to protect, to gather, to use, and to record information relevant to a forthcoming negotiation, and you may well find yourself one jump ahead of your bargaining buyers.

3. *Matching Concessions is Taboo*—Everybody wants to be liked. The problem is, this can get in the way of negotiations. If your buyer grants you a concession and you feel that the only gentlemanly thing to do is return the favor with an equal and matching concession, you may be guilty of poor negotiations practice. There are three disciplines to keep in mind in preparing your concession-making strategy:

- Discipline yourself to make small concessions in small chunks, and not just "split the difference."

- Discipline yourself not to make a big concession early in the bargaining, and certainly not a matching one.

- Discipline yourself to resist big concessions as the deadline approaches—and if the other party concedes big, do not respond with an equal concession.

- And most important, always ask for a concession in return *before* granting one.

If you anticipate your buyer offering a 5-cent-a-pound concession, plan to respond with a 1-cent-a-pound concession yourself, rather than meeting halfway. Be prepared to justify it—but whatever you do, do not base the level of your concession on the level of your buyer's concession.

One of the most critical points in the bargaining is to resist the propensity to make a major concession early-on when your buyer has made an exceptionally low offer, justifying it with information you were not aware of. Plan not to jump into an early major concession here, because first of all, you will have not yet tested the validity of his position. Secondly, you may enter into an unprofitable contract even if his information is valid.

If early big concessions are hazardous, late big concessions are even more so. The psychological pressure can be tremendous as a negotiation is getting right down to the wire. The point is to anticipate it and prepare to resist a major costly concession at the end by using alternatives such as a series of lesser concessions, or even a deadlock if acceptable.

4. *Ego Discipline*—In labor negotiations there is often an initial barrage of ego-bruising tactics to soften up the opponents and to tear down their expectations. This can happen in sales negotiations as well, but more often we see a quite different, and far more subtle—but equally effective—set of ploys. The point to remember is that whether you are tough-talked or sweet-talked by your prospective buyer, if he is a skilled negotiator he may simply be working on your ego. And if he has you psyched out with your guard down, it just may work. Three kinds of ego-related pitfalls to anticipate are:

a. The "smooth-as-silk" buyer or opponent.

b. The abusive negotiator.

c. Unexpected piques and clashes.

In preparing to deal effectively with these three areas, planning and anticipation are critical. Two efforts need to be pursued in advance to head off likely ego problems in the negotiation.

1. Make an advance list of the kinds of ego factors that might occur in a forthcoming negotiation.
2. Build any key items from your list into the role play sessions and preparatory discussion you hold prior to the negotiation.

If, for example, you think you are going to be up against a bunch of real pleasant "smoothies," who will try to flatter your people into submission, better get people on your team who are not susceptible to such ego-massaging. Try to recruit people who don't need that. If it is not practical to be that selective about who will be working with you in a given negotiation, and often it isn't, then for goodness sake conduct a briefing about your concerns over such ploys by your buyers. Prepare your "susceptibles" to ward off such tactics. A clever buyer may feel he can catch more flies with honey than with vinegar—and if your guys are not well-disciplined, he may do just that. Anticipate it. Practice how to deal with it. The same anticipation needs of course apply to the opponent who may attack you, or your team members', ego with some abusive barrage about your "lousy service," your "mediocre product," or your "crummy organization." Best select and prepare your fellow negotiators to deal with this sort of ploy with disciplined composure, possibly even returning his orneriness with sugar and sweetness.

It can even be useful to role-play some unexpected clashes or piqued egos, especially when preparing for a negotiation with a long-standing customer or business partner. One insecure or defensive negotiator on your side can set things back, and even cause irreparable damage to the bargaining, if through a brief misunderstanding he reacts in an ego-damaging way to the other side. The problem is there are certain "experts" (or bosses) who are difficult to eliminate from the bargaining team, but who may not be well-founded in the delicacies of human interactions. At the very least, even if you're stuck with such a quick-tempered person, you can prep him to anticipate these inevitable flashes of friction, and to plan a disciplined (and patient) reaction.

Indeed, why not make a checklist of discipline factors covering all four of the above areas in anticipation of every significant negotiation! You just never know what productive anticipatory results that might turn up.

We-They—We-They

One of the more useful exercises you can undertake before marching into a negotiation is to think through some likely scenarios of the proposals, responses, and counter-proposals. As is true with most planning and preparation, it is useful to involve your boss or other key people in that think-through. An example of some possible scenarios is plotted on page 51. The purpose is to anticipate the buyer's likely responses to various elements of a sales proposal, followed by the sellers best counter-proposals, and so on.

Here is how it works. In the left-hand column list the key elements; i.e., your opening targets, of an upcoming sales proposal. In the next column brainstorm the most likely responses the buyer might make to each of those opening elements. In our example there are just three likely responses to each, but there could be several. Once you have listed what you believe to be a representative list of all the buyer's likely responses to each of your opening elements, set up a third column to identify how you would respond to each of his responses. Continue the process into a fourth and fifth column or as far as you feel it is useful. If the negotiation involves more than one meeting, take a few minutes to go through this process just prior to each meeting. If the buyer is making the opening proposal, you would begin with his opening elements in the left-hand column, moving to your responses in the second column, and so on.

Rate Yourself on Your Negotiating Discipline

How effective are you at maintaining self-discipline throughout the pressures of the negotiation?

- Recognizing that the buyer has pressures too.
- Avoiding unnecessary concessions.
- Maintaining your cool under pressure.
- Taking time to listen and to think when time is short.
- Revising plans and strategies when appropriate.
- Discussing information protection with others in your organization.
- Testing the validity of new information.
- Keeping good records of the negotiation.
- Asking for larger concessions in return for your concessions.
- Controlling your ego with both "smoothies" and "nasties."
- Briefing others on your side to deal with "smoothies" and "nasties."
- Making a list of anticipated discipline factors.
- Engaging in a "we-they" think-through.

WE OPEN	THEY RESPOND	WE RESPOND	THEY RESPOND
$23/Unit	Too High OR $19/Unit OR They Accept	We've Had No Increase in 2 Years OR It's Going to $25 in January OR Celebrate	Can't Do Better—Deadlock OR Will Pay $20 if You Raise the Specs
Minimum 1000 units/order at 10 orders over one year	Too Much OR Minimum 144 units/order OR They Accept	Fixed Costs Make It Not Worth Commitment to Less OR Can Invoice Each 250 Units if Total Commitment OR Celebrate	Have to Do Better OR They Accept / Will Commit to 1000 if Will Invoice Each 144 Units OR They Accept
Specifications:			
A. 12 Stitches/Inch	Not Adequate OR 17 Stitches/Inch OR They Accept	Cost Based on 12— Cost Increase If More OR Celebrate	We'll Pay $22 if 15 Stitches
B. 4 Color Options	7 Color Options OR They Accept	Can Do if Raise Order Volume Proportionately OR Celebrate	Justify It
C. 500 lb. Test Strength	Inadequate OR 1000 lb. Test OR They Accept	Ask Why—How Are You Using It—Tell Us About Your Applications OR Celebrate	5% of End-User Customers Require High Performance

4

HOW TO PLAN
THE NEGOTIATING
CLIMATE

Key Customer:	"You've got one heck of a nerve coming in here to try to sell me something at a time like this! Boy, did you people ever screw me up! What I'm sending you back with is not a purchase order but a claim for $15,000."
Sales Rep:	"I heard about the problem, Perry. That's why I'm here. I think we can help get this sorted out."
Key Customer:	"Send me a check for $15,000. That will sort it out."
Sales Rep:	"Perry, you've been buying from us for over ten years. You know we won't damage you. You're a key account."
Key Customer:	"Cut the sales pitch. You've already damaged me."
Sales Rep:	"Perry, I grant you, we should have put the additional instruction labels on that shipment. But your night shift should never have tried to use our material in that kind of application."
Key Customer:	"Nonsense! How could they have known that?"
Sales Rep:	"Perry, I'm as concerned over your lost production run as you are. In fact, before we sort out your claim, could we talk about how to make sure this kind of problem never happens again?"
Key Customer:	pause.

Sales Rep: "How about it, Perry? Then I promise you we'll sort out the claim."

Key Customer: "Okay, okay. Sorry I'm so heated up over this."

Postscript: Perry ultimately recognized that it was his own people who had goofed. Our sales rep then was able to negotiate a nominal, face-saving claims payment in the form of some slightly off-spec inventory which Perry agreed to use in a less-demanding application.

PLANNING THE NEGOTIATING CLIMATE

What do we mean by "climate"? Well, it's sort of the feeling of calmness, storminess, smooth sailing, adverse elements, trouble-free conditions, sheer mayhem, and the like. The negotiating climate is created by your people and the other party's people in terms of the attitudes with which you approach each other in dealing with the key issues of the negotiation.

For purposes of sales negotiations there are three "climates" to consider. First is the "win-win" climate whereby both parties enter a negotiation with the intent of working for the best contract possible for both sides. Secondly, is the "win-lose" climate where each side intends to get all he can get at the expense of the other side. The third, and least common, is the "lose-win" where one side expects to sacrifice to the benefit of the other in order to help the other out of a tough situation. It is very important to think about what kind of climate you will be in when you go into a negotiation. The whole planning process for the negotiation will be molded by the sort of climate anticipated. If it is to be a win-win, then much of the preliminary fact-finding may well involve cooperative efforts by both sides to help each other understand problems and objectives, thereby permitting advance thinking about how to introduce ideas which help the other party at minimal sacrifice to you. If, however, a highly competitive win-lose attitude is expected, then sharing of information will probably not be in the plan. In fact protecting and concealing information is more likely.

The anticipated climate will dictate the strategies and tactics to be employed as well—aggressive versus patient exploration, pressure- and power-playing versus mutual problem-solving.

The climate can shift during a negotiation. If one side starts out in a win-win attitude and the other in a win-lose, either the patient persuasiveness of the "wins" or the intransigence of the "loses" is going to prevail and the climate will shift in one direction or the other. A negotiation can begin with a win-win attitude by both sides, but if one begins to lose faith in the other side's willingness to give and take on a mutual basis the climate can easily drift into a win-lose. Therefore, it is useful to anticipate what kinds of things could cause a shift and prepare to deal with them if they occur.

Sales-pro Joe Nathanial and his design engineers of the Smoother Systems Company had made their opening proposal to Tuff-Nut Buyers, Inc. only to have the Tuff-Nut representatives respond with a totally irrational counter-offer accompanied by abusive statements about Smoother System's capabilities and pricing policies. Joe and his engineers diplomatically dealt with Tuff-Nut's next series of barrages against their proposal, and their organization, and ever so gently began to move the conversation into probing for *specific* problem-solving opportunities that would be useful to Tuff-Nut. They discovered an inexpensive design change that could save Tuff-Nut over $7,000 a year. They discovered that it would be acceptable to raise the monthly service fees slightly if the initial equipment cost could be lowered, resulting in a "wash" in the total cost. And they found a way to reword the proposal to give the Tuff-Nut people a more palatable package to present to their management. Joe and his engineers had walked into an aggressive, win-lose-oriented buyer, and through patient problem-solving had converted the bargaining process into a win-win.

That is not to suggest that all win-lose situations can be converted, nor that there are not times when it is your intent to generate a win-lose situation with you on the winning end. It is important to think through in advance which climate you want to be in and which climate your opponent is apt to foster early-on. If you expect the two sides to coincide in the climate intended, then plan how to keep it that way. But, if you anticipate the need to convert the climate to a win-win, expect to use a great deal of patience, or if to a win-lose (you win), whatever tactics are necessary to gain the upper hand.

The Win-Lose Climate

When would a win-lose climate be appropriate? After all, aren't we striving for good business partnerships, long-range working relationships, and reputations as good people to do business with? Well yes, but the problem is the other guy isn't always thinking that way.

Your buyer might be under such pressure from his organization that you know his very survival may depend on getting an agreement from you at a totally unacceptable level. In this case he is going to force you into a win-lose situation whether you like it or not. Or, you may be trying to sell to a government agency whose practices and procedures almost force you into getting everything you can for your side. You may be in very difficult times, and for your survival or your company's survival, the buyer can pressure you into a good deal for him. It may be a one-time customer and neither of you particularly care about the long-range relationship. Let's face it, there are times when you will be in highly competitive climates where for whatever reason, one party is going to gain at the other's expense. So it's best to be prepared for it both psychologically and factually so as to be on the win side of the win-lose negotiation.

The strategies and the tactics you will be preparing for a win-lose negotiation are significantly different from those you would plan for in the win-win. They are based on a completely different set of assumptions. Because of this, strategies and tactics should not be planned until the expected climate conditions have been defined.

B & B Engineering Company was about to bid on a subcontract to provide the fluid control systems to a large firm who had the prime contract for a major processing installation. Although B & B had done work before on an amicable basis with this same prime contractor, they discovered through the grape-vine that there had been some heavy cost overruns on another part of the contract. This meant that their negotiating opponents would probably be under heavy pressure to strike as good a deal as possible on this particular subcontract. In their past joint efforts B & B had made it a practice to share certain design information with the prime contractor to facilitate overall planning. But this time around the prime contractor seemed almost overanxious to get their hands on advance data. Putting two and two together, B & B concluded that they were about to be confronted with a win-lose negotiation—that the pressure would be on, and that they had better start thinking right then and there about what strategies and tactics to employ. One of the strategies they selected was to protect their design information. This proved to be very wise for as it turned out they did face an aggressive negotiating opponent, and they would have been forced to sacrifice a sizeable chunk of their profit margin had they revealed certain efficiencies they had been able to introduce into the fluid systems design.

The focus of a win-lose negotiating climate is on power. The image you attempt to create, and prevent your opponents from taking, is that of holding the trump card, of being in control and having something the other side needs more than you need to part with it. Thus, the climate to be created is one in which you will ultimately be able to exploit the other party's perceived weaknesses. That is not to suggest that a win-lose climate necessarily carries a hostile set of attitudes. If their weakness is their need for praise and other ego-building measures, your attitude may well be very complimentary on the surface but with the overall intent of exploiting their weaknesses and gaining a power position.

The Limited but Important Lose-Win Climate

There are circumstances where in the short run your organization is willing to take a gamble to help a new customer get off the ground or help an old one out of a bind. The climate you establish early in the negotiation will be a highly cooperative one. In this case it will be useful to convey to the other party the full extent of the risk and the sacrifice you are taking on their behalf, without holding a knife to the throat for a long-term commitment. Not that you wouldn't expect to press a hard bargain with certain types of "risk" customers, but that it begins to verge on the win-lose if you plan to push their backs to the wall.

Factors to Think About in a Win-Win Climate

If you are in the business of negotiating sales contracts and agreements with organizations who are important to you in the long range, then clearly you need to consider establishing win-win climates. It can be done, and is done every day—where two parties work closely together to find better ways to strike a bargain to the advantage of both.

1. *Establishing Long-Range Relationships.* The more the buyer or customer or contractor knows about your operation and problems, the more he can offer money-saving or time-saving suggestions, like modifying his specs slightly to give you some major benefit. The more your organization knows about the customer, the more useful suggestions your people can make to help accommodate his needs.

This suggests the value in a cooperative exchange of information and ideas, and they do not flow freely without a certain degree of faith and trust. B will not confide in A if in the past A has used B's information to gain an advantage over B.

If you are a sole source supplier, the buyer needs you. But if you are fair and equitable in dealing with that buyer, he may well be able to share information with you to the benefit of both. He's not apt to share information if he fears you may use it to raise your price or lower your quality. If you plan to establish a win-win climate, communicate that to him, and maintain that posture, and it can indeed serve the two of you well.

Are there any disadvantages to a win-win climate? There can be risks if the other side is not sincere, or if there is high turnover in their negotiating team. But that may simply suggest a more ardent effort to establish climate. The only other major disadvantage is that it may take a long time to establish that climate, time which is not available on a given negotiation.

"But we can't establish a winning climate with those dudes, they have no credibility."—"Oh, why not?" you say. "Well, we don't know them, and you know how competitive these wholesalers are."—"Yes, but we want them to handle our stuff for a good long time in this area, so why can't we at least start out in a genuine and friendly way with them?"—"They'll take us for a ride. This is Brooklyn you know, and everybody from Brooklyn is like that!" But you respond very calmly, "Well let's try it this way first anyway, because we need to build some credibility too you know."

2. *Converting a Doubtful or Aggressive Buyer.* If you have determined that a win-win climate would be the most appropriate in a given negotiation, but the other side comes at you like a bulldog, your first thrust should be to win them over. You may realize that there are some ways you can help each other, ways that the other side is not aware of. Make them aware. Focus on the areas you believe you can help them with. Draw out the facts and offer some solutions or hints of solutions; i.e., ideas that communicate to your buyers that a mutual problem-solving approach can be beneficial to them. Not every win-lose-oriented buyer can, nor should, be converted. But to not even make the attempt when you believe the benefits are there may result in many a lost opportunity.

3. *Seeking a Better Bargain for Everybody.* In addition to faith and trust it takes work. Here are a few examples just to illustrate some potential benefits:

- You discover that you could realize a significant cost savings by delivering 5,000 units instead of the 2,000 the buyer wants, and that he is willing to take 5,000 if you'll share the savings with him.
- You learn that the customer does not need an auxiliary item, and that he is willing to share the savings with you if your production people will leave it off.

- The contractor wants a penalty clause in the contract for delayed delivery of materials. You are under pressure from your management to resist this due to uncertain common carrier services during the critical delivery time period. However, having established a good working relationship with the contractor, you discover that he is willing to provide some of his trucks to you and that in turn your engineering group can give him some vital technical assistance at the time of startup. This swap solves both your problems and facilitates a $7 million deal.

- You learn through an informal mutual problem-solving discussion that if you will lower your base contract price, the buyer will agree to purchase some extra services at a price which will more than make up for the reduction in the base.

- You discover that the other organization needs some temporary financing in order to agree to your proposal, that they are not aware that you can arrange that financing, and that they have an excellent credit rating.

4. *Mutual Goal-Setting.* It may help your organization to take advantage of some economic opportunities if you are aware of a particular customer's long-term objectives. This could in turn permit you to grant some benefits to that customer. The trouble is, neither the customer nor yourselves will know this if you aren't familiar with each other's longer-range goals. A win-win climate will facilitate an exchange of information which can generate some mutually beneficial adjustments and tradeoffs in your long-range goals and planning.

5. *Problem-Solving.* Both sides of a negotiation will have some problems which the other side can help solve. Before the solutions flow, the climate has to be right. Problem-solving in negotiations has to be a two-way street.

6. *The Key Is Homework.* Establishing effective long-range working relationships requires a lot of effort. You need to know a lot about the other organization, tapping as many resources as possible for information and background. Information triggers creative ideas and creative ideas are needed to convert win-lose oriented opponents and to find better bargains for both sides. Homework needs to be coordinated and needs to include everybody involved in the negotiating climate. If you can arrange for your engineers and your market researchers and accountants to communicate with their engineers, market researchers, or accountants long before the hard bargaining begins, that process of mutual goal-setting and mutual problem-solving becomes as natural as signing the contract.

7. *Team Makeup.* In thinking about building the conditions for a win-win climate, it is critical to select members of the negotiating team not only for their content knowledge but also for their ability to function in a cooperative give-and-take environment. On the other side of the coin, a totally different type of team member might be selected for a very competitive tug-of-war kind of negotiation. Here again, in the task of selecting the negotiating team, it is useful to think through what sort of climate is apt to exist. In many lengthy complex negotiations both sides fully intend to start out in a tough stance giving the appearance of a win-lose, but with the expectation of winding up in a win-win finale when the ultimate agreement is reached. In such cases it may be necessary to plan replacing your "tough guy" team members midway through the bargaining with some more "reasonable" types in order to move the climate towards a mutual problem-solving basis once the more difficult issues have been bargained. In fact a climate shift of this sort is probably more common than either the pure win-lose or win-win.

8. *Individual Needs.* However complex and however difficult a sales or contract negotiation may be, as a professional sales negotiator never forget that you are dealing with individual egos. To establish the winning climate the needs of these individual egos must be taken into account in the planning. It takes longer to establish credibility, faith, and trust with an opponent who's been burned before, or who's under pressure, than one who has not been subjected to these forces.

The surest way to destroy a good climate is to say or do something which the other party interprets as a blow to his ego. Failure to compliment him on something he indicates pride over—e.g., his bragging about his experience in this industry—can be a missed opportunity. Using the wrong humor at the wrong time—e.g., kidding an insecure purchasing agent about an oversight while in the company of his boss—can be a missed opportunity. Indirectly criticizing something the buyer values—e.g., his industry's methodology, regulatory matters, etc.—can cost many negotiating points. Thus, in planning the climate you desire, it is useful to make a list of the turn-ons and turn-offs to be considered with each key personality on the opposing team.

9. *Assumptions.* "You know, that guy Smith may not be too swift technically, so even though we want to maintain a good rapport I don't think he'll be bothered too much if we reduce that tolerance." "These guys are hurting financially, so let's not bend an inch on the terms."

"Look, they don't offer us anything in the long range so we'll give them a take-it-or-leave-it proposal." "They're bluffing Jack, they don't need this stuff till November." "They're going to be more trouble than they're worth, so don't waste too much effort on them."

How about those assumptions for kicking off a win-win climate?

You just never know how much value a particular customer or buyer might be until you've tested your assumptions—tested them with more and better information. Maybe your assumptions are true, but test them first.

10. *Discipline*. Remember, a win-win climate does not mean a soft-soap or coddling climate! It means a mutually cooperative, hard-working climate. It never reduces your primary responsibility to gain the best deal possible for your organization. This requires discipline. And an essential part of discipline is effective planning. The discipline of considering each of the above factors in planning your negotiating climate, particularly the win-win, can pay heavy dividends in your long-term success. Plan your climate before you plan the strategies and tactics. Be prepared to deal with the need to shift climate during a negotiation, and be prepared to deal with one that shifts whether you want it to or not. And finally, prepare to discipline yourself and your support people to deal with the appropriate climate.

A Win-Win Checklist

What can I do to enhance a long-range relationship with this buyer organization?

What can I do to convert this skeptical buyer to a win-win climate?

What opportunities are there for a better bargain for both of us?

How can I initiate a mutual goal-setting approach with this buyer?

What problem-solving opportunities are there with this buyer?

How can we cooperate in helping each other do our homework?

Who are the best people in my organization to join-in in fostering a win-win relationship with this buyer organization?

Who are the key players in the buyer organization, and what are their individual ego needs?

What assumptions are we making which could interfere with a win-win climate?

What do we need to address in our own self-discipline to assure that this win-win climate results in productive outcomes?

Rate Yourself as a Climate-Setter

How effective are you at establishing and maintaining an appropriate negotiating climate?

- Picking the appropriate climate to carry into the negotiation.
- Patiently converting a win-lose climate into a win-win.
- Protecting yourself in a win-lose climate when necessary.
- Recognizing, and accepting, a win-lose climate when it is inevitable.
- Adapting your strategies and tactics to the appropriate climate.
- Recognizing a win-lose climate in spite of friendly and courteous behaviors.
- Employing a lose-win climate when appropriate.
- Establishing a feeling of faith and trust with your long-time customers.
- Proving the benefits of win-win to an aggressive buyer.
- Finding win-win tradeoffs that benefit both sides.
- Getting key customers to share long-range goals.
- Managing a mutual exchange of helpful information.
- Getting the right people involved to enhance a long-range relationship.
- Testing potentially damaging assumptions.
- Maintaining a disciplined perspective about your win-win relationships.

5

HOW TO DESIGN STRATEGIES, TACTICS, AND COUNTER-TACTICS BEFORE YOU MEET TO NEGOTIATE

Sales Rep:	"I can sell you this cutter for $100."
Customer:	"That's too much, you'll have to reduce it."
Sales Rep:	"Fred is the only one who could reduce it, and he's gone for three weeks. I doubt he'd reduce it anyway."
Customer:	"But I need it now. Besides, this is only 24-inch. I need 36-inch."
Sales Rep:	"What kinds of jobs will you use it on?"
Customer:	"Mostly routine. But every now and then I need a wide cut."
Sales Rep:	"We have one 30-inch cutter back here I can let you have for $120."
Customer:	"That's too expensive."
Sales Rep:	"Tell you what. If you'll reset these mounts yourself, I can reduce it to $115."
Customer:	"Okay. But only if that includes the frame."
Sales Rep:	"I'd love to include the frame, but Fred would have a fit."
Customer:	"But I gotta have a frame. Look, my van is about to leave. How about it?"

Sales Rep: "Let's do this. I'll include the frame, and extra kit of bolts, and two cans of lubricant; all for only an additional $15, which gives you a total price of only $130."

Customer: "Still sounds high, but I guess I'll take it."

Sales Rep: "I wouldn't sell it for that, but you're one of our higher quality customers."

DESIGNING STRATEGIES, TACTICS, AND COUNTER-TACTICS

Negotiation strategies and tactics are so directly related to objectives and climate that only after these two latter areas have been thought through is it desirable to plot out *how* to get to your end results. It's like not selecting your plays until you know what sort of a defense you are up against, and what condition the players are in.

You would not put together a game plan before watching game films and analyzing the scouting reports. You cannot negotiate effectively without information. Because without information you cannot assemble effective strategies and tactics. Especially if you are in a team negotiation! And you would certainly not go into either a game or a negotiation without a plan. A plan must include strategies; e.g., "What information are we going to dig out of these people?" or "What decision steps do we need to lead them through?" It must also include some attention to tactics; e.g., "Let Tom ask this set of questions since he can put more pressure on their technical expertise" or "We'll get up and walk out if they refuse Item G."

A strategy is a positioning approach or a general order of maneuvering; whereas, a tactic is a specific action within a strategy.

Basing Your Strategies on Strengths

It can be productive to have a brainstorming type approach, getting several inputs into your list of bargaining strengths. Your *key people* can be a source of bargaining strength due to their reputation in their field, their experience, or their contacts. *Technology* is a major source of bargaining strength as long as its benefits can be directly tied to the plans and needs of the other organization. If *time* is on your side, it becomes a major bargaining strength and should make a decided impact on how you plan to pace the negotiation. Your potential for future impact on the other organization, due to *planned developments* could be a source of bargaining strength depending on the timing. *Financial* aspects are, of course, a major area of strength if you can either build for less or help the buyer spend less in using your products or services. *Location* may be a strength for ready access reasons. And, not least, the direct design factors built into your *product or service* can often be a major source of bargaining strength.

A second area in planning your strategies is the need to list your weaknesses as well. And you do have some. They may be in any of the areas listed above, and whatever strategies you design must be worked around those weaknesses.

Listing Strengths of the Buyer

A third area of consideration in strategy planning is the strengths of the other guys. Are they in bed with your tougher *competitors?* Do they always seem to have better *information* than you? Is *timing* or future *developments* on their side? Do they have other strong *alternatives,* and are they *better planners* than your organization is? In short, do they have more strengths than your side?

The fourth area to look at in strategy formulation is the weaknesses of the other side. And they have some too, if you look for them.

Setting Negotiation Strategies

Begin with a set of objectives, and chart a course over one of these three routes:

Win—Win— you and the buyer both gain.
Win—Lose—you gain at the buyer's expense.
Lose—Win—you sacrifice, letting the buyer win (to bail him out of difficulty, or to set up a longer-term objective)

In most business negotiations the win-win strategy is clearly the more intelligent one to pursue over the long pull. It involves mutual concern, joint problem-solving, and occasionally short-term sacrifice. But it pays off many times in the long run.

Time and team makeup are two things which are critical to keep in mind in setting negotiating strategies. A clear understanding must be established of the final date acceptable for agreement. From that date you can work backwards with your strategy planning to determine when it might be useful to walk out of the negotiation in an attempt to put pressure on the opponent (and still have time to consummate an agreement). It is also critical to plan each team member's role in the strategy selected. Will your senior member be kept out of the hard bargaining until the very end? Will the financial people be brought in at a particular point? And who will play the key role of problem-solver and moderator?

Five Strategic Questions

In thinking through the flow of your negotiating strategy, there are five strategic questions worth asking. Why has this buyer organization elected to negotiate with us? What should the shape of our concession curve look like? What are the timing issues in this negotiation? Who are the key players? Where is the best place to negotiate? Let's examine each of these in a bit more depth.

- *Why Has This Buyer Organization Elected to Negotiate with Us?*—There is not always a clear-cut line between their decision to buy from you and their bargaining with you for the best possible deal. But once they do engage you in serious negotiation, there is a fair chance they believe that your product or service is what they need. So what strategies are implied by their initial negotiating attitude? Does it appear that they definitely want to reach an agreement, and that you are probably the only seller they are negotiating with on this particular purchase? Or are they just shopping at this point? Do they seem to be taking a cooperative problem-solving approach, or are they testing you with some hardball tactics? Based on that, what information had you better gather (and protect) both before and during any more serious give-and-take discussion?

    Probing for information that tells you why they've chosen to negotiate with you will guide you along the most productive course throughout the negotiation.

- *What Should the Shape of Our Concession Curve Look Like?*—If more sellers would just think about this one ahead of time, they would probably give more small concessions when necessary to keep the negotiation alive, and fewer large concessions which are often unnecessary. To picture the desired concession curve in your mind, you first need to have a clear fix on your objectives, both in terms of your highest expectations and your lowest acceptable, or mandatory, levels. Your primary objective may be price, or it may be something else. Your concession curve must be based on your primary objective. The tradeoffs you are willing to use should then be based mainly on your other objectives, those which you will be willing to offer concessions on in order to sustain a firm concession curve on that primary objective. Some of those other objectives, (e.g., specifications, delivery, etc.) may also be too important to give in on easily, so you need a third level of "throw away" concessions to use as tradeoffs. And the sooner you can clearly understand the buyer's objectives, the sooner you can begin to manage your concessions intelligently. Of course you may never know what the buyer's best case and worst case objectives are. So the key is not to give unilateral or big concessions. Go into your negotiations with a mind set to always ask for a concession in return, and to give small concessions when necessary.

Now the above may all sound like a win-lose type strategy. Not necessarily. Even in a win-win problem-solving negotiation, with a very good customer, there is a risk in making big concessions too early without exploring possible tradeoffs. The whole point in win-win strategies is to examine ways both sides can help each other to arrive at the best outcome possible. Since this process takes time, it is useful to keep your buyer motivated by proving to him that as he suggests ideas that are helpful to you, you will reciprocate with concessions and alternatives that benefit him.

- *What Are the Timing Issues in This Negotiation?*—When is the best time to negotiate with this buyer? Tuesday morning? Friday afternoon? The month before his budget is due? This is closely related to your concession curve strategy. The pacing of concessions and tradeoffs is vitally affected by time constraints and perceived time value. Do you expect this negotiation to conclude today, or will it continue over several meetings and phone conversations? What deadlines are there on either the buyer or yourselves?

  If time is on the buyer's side, should you try to create earlier deadlines by limiting the time period for which your offer is available? What other factors can you bring to bear that will relieve time pressure on you, or increase it a bit on the buyer?

- *Who Are the Key Players?*—As sellers we often focus too much of our attention on that one buyer we deal with face-to-face, and not enough on other people who will impact the negotiation. What do we know about that buyer, his style, his organization, and how he and his organization interact? What are his personal goals and ego needs that we should attend to to keep this negotiation on track? And are there third parties who could be influencing this negotiation in our favor?

  Once you understand who the key influencers are, you can then adjust the mix on your own side to make sure the right people in your organization are saying the right things to the right people in the buyer organization. It may be higher management, or it may be a technical person who is the key to moving the discussion along in your favor.

- *Where Is the Best Place to Negotiate?*—Typically you conduct your sales negotiations at the buyer's location, and you don't have much choice in the matter. But it is still useful to ask yourself the above question. Negotiating on their turf may well be the best place, since it could give

you access to their behind-the-scenes influences, to their higher approval levels, and to nuggets of information about their needs and
intentions you could not get anywhere else. But, if you could get them
to come to your location, it could put more time pressure on them, leave
them with less access to information details, and enable you to control
the setting and the agenda. Or maybe the best place of all would be a
neutral location where everybody is away from the firing line and can
concentrate on the negotiation. When someone takes the time and
trouble to make a trip to another location, it indicates they are just a
little more committed to concluding a satisfactory deal.

So those are the five key strategic questions you need to ask
yourself, and your support people, as you approach any sales negotiation. Whether it will be a 30-minute or a 30-week negotiation,
examining these questions will help you to position yourself strate-
gically. You will then be able to pick and choose the best tactics to
fulfill the appropriate strategies. Even a short discussion with your
boss or key support persons, addressing these questions, can pay
healthy dividends. For as you move into tactics, it's best to remember,
there is no good tactic for a bad strategy.

How to Prepare Tactics

- *Opening Demands*—The more knowledge you have, and the better you
  have done your homework, the more prepared you are to lead off the
  bargaining with your opening demands. If you are confident that your
  targets are high but realistic, and you know what strategy you intend to
  pursue, then prepare to strike first. This is a general rule, and there
  are exceptions, particularly in more complex negotiations or when a
  certain protocol must be followed. But in most cases, plan to take the
  initiative. There are, on the other hand, situations where you have not
  been able to gather the information you need to open with confidence.
  If this is the case, and you know you must elicit some critical
  information during the face-to-face discussions, then be prepared to
  adjust your strategies accordingly as soon as the data you need comes
  out.
     The other side may well be in a stronger opening position and
  attempt to take the lead with an opening offer before you are in
  position to assess their bargaining strengths and weaknesses. If so, plan
  to be patient, to acknowledge this offer, but to hold firm until you are
  able to assess the situation with some useable information. The point is,
  in planning your tactics, match the blank spots in your planning sheets
  and checklists with the information you need to gather during the

negotiation. Then be prepared to add to, or modify, your strategies and tactics as tentatively planned. In planning to respond to any opening offer, one rule always to follow is—Do *not* let their opening offer lower your intended target!

Even if their opening offer is so low that it tends to make you question the reality of your original targets, *do not* lower them at this early point in the negotiation.

- *Authority Levels*—In anticipating how to react to any request the buyer may make in a given negotiation, it is useful to consider responding with "I don't have the authority to grant that concession." If that is a tactic you build into your plan, it is important that everybody on your negotiating team understands how and when the tactic will be used. Pleading "no authority" can be a powerful tactic to evade pressure situations, but everybody has to be on-board.

  The fact that the "no authority" tactic can be so effective suggests that in preparing to negotiate, it is oftentimes useful to try to arrange to negotiate with the highest level possible in the other organization. This reduces their ability to rely on the same tactic. Take this sequence for example. You are preparing to negotiate with the purchasing engineer at Isolated Products Company. It occurs to you that her contract authority is probably no more than $10,000. Your objective is to negotiate a series of contracts for a three-year period, including a service contract. The total value of this is nearly $70,000. Automatically the purchasing engineer is going to be able to use the "no authority" tactic on you. Thus, if you can arrange to involve her Director of Engineering (or even a Vice-President) in the bargaining, you have a chance of defusing the "no authority" tactic. On the other hand, the more you can avoid bringing along your "heavy breathers," the more you can plan to fall back on "no authority" as the other side begins to press you for expensive modifications to your proposal. That is not to suggest that this, or any other tactic, is always appropriate. But in your planning think it through. Consider it as a possibility.

- *Information Tactics*—There are two ways you might plan to use this one. If you anticipate some heavy pressure by your buyers to make some key concessions, plan to ask for a recess until you can gather some additional data "back at the shop." Like the "no authority" tactic, this can be particularly useful if you have time on your side and the other guys are under time pressure to reach an agreement. Of course, if you haven't done your homework you might not be aware of this. Another application of the "information" tactic is to plan to put pressure on the buyer for more information to justify a concession he is requesting. "Jim, we may be able to modify our proposed packaging, but we need to have your engineers run some tests on how these corner binding changes will affect durability in your new conveyor system."

- *Tough Guy Tactics*—You may be anticipating a difficult negotiation, but as the salesperson you do not want to engage in heated exchange which could jeopardize your long-term relationship with the account. This is the time you need to arrange to bring somebody else with you to play the "tough guy" role. It can be an accountant, a boss, a technical type—anybody who could be "almost unreasonable" in standing firm against heavy pressure to make concessions. There is some risk in knowing when to get your "tough guy" removed from the bargaining before damage is done. But with anticipation, perceptiveness, and a clear signal planned between the two of you, this can be done. Once your "tough guy" is withdrawn it can be much easier for you to come out like the hero, making much smaller concessions than you could have gotten away with otherwise.

- *Changing the Package*—Plan in advance what changes you can offer as inexpensive concessions to sweeten the package for the buyer. You might change the design in ways that help him but cost you little. You might change the delivery schedule to make it more convenient for him with little inconvenience to you. Or you may be able to alter the payment terms and schedule to help him take advantage of everything from inventory tax breaks to budget period advantages; all with minimal cost to you.

- *Peddling Some Extras*—One tactic frequently used in planning to gain a bit of additional value is to sell some extras after the main part of the deal is basically agreed upon. This becomes especially important if you anticipate having to make some expensive concessions in order to get the sale or the contract. For example, you may push for a service contract or a supplier contract, either of which may carry a high potential net profit as compared to the main contract. You may push to sell training services for employees of your buyer, helping them to use your product or service more effectively. You may offer consulting service add-ons, again at a high net profit. You may be able to provide marketing or promotional support that could be useful to the buyer. The fact is your negotiations plan should include the "peddling some extras" tactic to assure that any inexpensive-sounding (but high net profit) add-ons are tacked on at the end.

- *Diversion Tactics*—In a highly competitive negotiation, where you are a bit light in bargaining strengths or heavy in weaknesses, it may be useful to divert your opponent's attention by introducing all the data, statistics, and graphs at your command. You can also play on his ego by complimenting his reasoning and the soundness of his requests: "If only you had the wherewithal to accommodate him at this time." Other diversions such as government regulations, safety requirements, procedures, policies, preprinted contracts (anything preprinted may give the appearance of credibility), etc., should be considered in planning of tactics to employ should the pressure get heavy.

- *Changing People Tactics*—In preparing what to do if negotiations get bogged down, one tactic worth considering is changing negotiators. For example, you may judge that initially your lead negotiator should be an engineering type in order to get agreement on some difficult technical aspects of the proposal. But once that stage of the negotiation is completed, you may want to shift gears and send a sales type in to shift the emphasis to building personal relationships. Following that, you may plan to send the hard-nosed bargainer in to drive home the hard bargains. The important thing is not where you draw the line between the definition of "strategy" and "tactic," but that you consider in advance the desirability of changing negotiators or team members according to preplanned actions.

- *Time-Related Tactics*—You can, and should, plot out in advance the expected timing issues of the negotiation and the appropriate pacing tactics you intend to employ in dealing with those issues. As discussed previously, it is important to determine when you must conclude the negotiation, and work backwards from there. Only then will you be able to plan when to be patient, when to purposely stall or speed-up the bargaining, and when to make concessions.

The most critical tactic in negotiations planning has to do with the rate at which you will make concessions. The rule, which should be inscribed on the inside of your forehead, is *"Plan to concede in very small pieces and very, very slowly, if you must concede at all."*

A second important time-related tactic is planned deadlock. Provided time is on your side, and provided you feel that effective pressure can result, you may well decide in advance to reach a deadlock with the buyer if he fails to accept your asking price (and conditions) within a preplanned time period. This tactic would only be used if the risk was not unreasonable. You cannot always plan when the opportune time will occur, but you must plan when and if you are willing to deadlock to sustain a firm price. One device which can be helpful in planning this is to draw a line graph indicating the rate at which you are willing to make and seek concessions over points on which you would be willing to temporarily deadlock, as a tactic to put pressure on the other side.

A perfectly valid tactic to plan to employ when you are under pressure, or being outmanned, is to call time-out. The more formal the negotiation, the more you should plan to do this. This is particularly true in team negotiations where you see a need to talk things over, to let somebody cool off, or to slow down the pace.

There are times when you would like to negotiate something as quickly as possible. In simpler negotiating situations, you might even do your bargaining by telephone, with a fast-moving checklist kind of approach, designed to get a commitment from the buyer before he has time to establish resistance or think of a counter-offer. You may also find situations in which you need to reach an agreement before all the necessary information is available, thus calling for a signing of the agreement now, with the understanding that certain terms and conditions will have to be negotiated later.

The final time-related tactic to plan on is patience. Patience can be critical, particularly when you sense that a buyer or buyer team is having problems negotiating internally with their own organization people or with each other, and time is needed before they will be in position to make a commitment.

• *Ego-Building Tactics*—If the buyer is put into a position where he feels that he has lost face, particularly with his own organization, or if he feels that you have bruised his ego, he is going to somehow attempt to strike back. Whether he does it now or later, and whether he is successful or not, you will not benefit and you stand to lose in the long run. In planning negotiations, make an effort to have some ego-building tactics in your kit.

There are many ways to do this. Pay a compliment regarding his own credibility, his organization, his team's proposal, or anything else that may relieve pressure on him while you are standing firm on the bargaining issues.

There may be ways you can help him to present your offer to his management in a more palatable form. Timing and subtlety can be critical in offering bait that he can use to feed his ego while justifying an otherwise less than ideal package to his management, in a form which appears that he has struck a good bargain. For every dollar you gain in economic value, plan to give your buyer a dollar's worth of ego value in return.

Preparing Counter-Tactics

Although a win-win strategy is the more intelligent in long range business relationships, you clearly have to be prepared to deal with the tactics of a win-lose oriented buyer. Even in win-win negotiations, it is the responsibility of both you and your buyer to employ tactics which will assure a positive outcome for your respective organizations. Thus, it is vital to plan to use counter-tactics when you are about to deal with skilled negotiators. There are four basic steps to take in preparing your counter-tactics.

1. *List the buyer's likely tactics.* If the buyer organization is skilled, they will probably plan to open with a very low offer, and will intend to concede

very conservatively. If the strength of your proposal puts pressure on them, they may plead no authority, especially if they can afford a time delay more than you can. They may plan to inundate you with financial or technical data. They may send a "tough guy" at you to soften you up for a "nice guy" to make the kill. They may plan to demand certain changes in the package once you've made some basic commitments. And they may ask for the extras gratis before you have a chance to sell them once the basic sale is finalized. They may hit you with a variety of diversionary tactics and even change negotiators on you just about the time you think you have it wrapped up. If they sense that you are under time pressure, they may employ all sorts of stalling tactics. If the reverse is true, they may try to hurry you into a rush deal loaded in their favor. And finally, they may be so skilled as to make you feel good all over having given-away-the-shop.

2. *Prepare your counter-tactics.* After you have made a list of any of the above tactics you think the buyers might employ, get your team together and brainstorm a list of counter-tactics you will employ if needed. For example, if there is a wide gap between your opening price and the buyer's opening offer, plan how you will move the bargaining into an information-gathering state without forcing a deadlock right off the bat. If they plead no authority on one of your demands, plan in advance how you might counter by offering to break that demand into smaller units (within their direct authority levels), or to press for a meeting with the appropriate authority level. Preparation is the key to countering unexpected financial, technical, or marketing information. It is especially important to know how to discriminate between valid and relevant information as opposed to a flood of useless decoy type data. The same goes for assessing any rationale the buyer may offer for making expensive changes to the package as you originally proposed it. Counter-tactics to deal with the "tough guy" on the buyer's team, or to the sudden change in negotiators, may need to be patience, may be deadlock, or may be asking for something in return. Whatever tactic they employ, there is an appropriate counter-tactic. It needs to be thought through in advance, particularly as it relates to your time constraints. In planning to counter the myriad of diversion tactics, or the pressing for expensive extras your buyer might attempt, brainstorm with your team or other knowledgeable people in advance to list the tactics you are likely to be faced with, and what to do about them if confronted. If you are under less time pressure than the buyer, your primary counter-tactic can be patience. If the tables are turned, the skill with which you plan how to counter a slow-down, a time-out, an impending deadlock, and a very patient opponent, will be crucial. And finally, be prepared to deal with the negotiator who snows you with compliments, for you must first

plan to apply the counter-tactics to your own ego before you can neutralize those ego-building tactics he will be showering upon you.

3. *Establish your team roles.* Once you have a list of likely tactics the other guys may employ, and a list of appropriate counter-tactics, your next step is to assign the responsibility, for carrying out those counter-tactics, to specific people on your negotiating team. For example, if they pull the bit of proposing expensive changes in the package, you may want to assign the role of planning counter-proposals to an engineering type or a financial whiz. If a long-range working relationship is important, the role(s) *you* assume must be one of strength, but not one of belligerence.

Much of the effect of counter-tactics is a result of the decisiveness with which they are employed. And decisiveness can be greatly enhanced by effective role assignment and proper planning.

4. *Role-play your counter-tactics.* Despite all the good planning, and astute attention to role preparation, it can all go to pot if not properly executed when time comes for the "live" negotiation. One of the best ways to assure effective execution is to practice.

By practice we mean "dry run" or "role play" some mock negotiating sessions with your team. Get some old pros, or some knowledgeable devil's advocates, to assume the role of your upcoming buyers. Have them hit you with some tactics to which you and your team can respond.

Prepare a Written Plan

Whether you are attempting to sell a $10,000 supply contract or a $10 million construction contract, it is vital to put your strategy and tactics preparations in writing—even if it's nothing more than a highlight outline for you and your boss, or subordinate, to talk through. Make it visible to all concerned. This permits a better chance of pinpointing pitfalls, preparation gaps, and bargaining opportunities. Begin by listing in priority order your side's bargaining strengths and weaknesses (two separate lists) and your buyer's strengths and weaknesses.

Follow that with a description of your basic strategies, based on those strengths and weaknesses. Then list the tactics you plan to employ at key points in the negotiation. Do another list of tactics your buyer may employ. Alongside each of those tactics, list appropriate counter-tactics, and who is responsible for planning and executing each counter-tactic.

Add this part of your overall negotiating plan to your Objectives and Targets and Information Needs sections, and you are well on your way to an effective negotiation.

Checklist of Negotiating Tactics

OPENING DEMANDS
  Strike first.
  Acknowledge theirs, and hold firm.

AUTHORITY LEVELS
  Plead no authority.
  Negotiate at their highest level.
  Avoid bringing your higher authorities.

INFORMATION TACTICS
  Recess to gather more information.
  Demand justification.

TOUGH GUY TACTICS
  Use a support person to force a tough issue.

CHANGING THE PACKAGE
  Offer inexpensive changes and concessions.

PEDDLING SOME EXTRAS
  Sell some "little" high profit extras at the end.

DIVERSION TACTICS
  Use "I'd like to but…"

CHANGING PEOPLE TACTICS
  Change the pace with a different negotiator.

TIME-RELATED TACTICS
  Use patience.
  Use small, slowly paced concessions.
  Use planned (temporary) deadlocks.
  Call time-out.
  Use a fast-paced checklist.
  Give the other side time to sort things out.

EGO-BUILDING TACTICS
  Help the buyer save face.
  Stroke the buyer's ego.
  Make the buyer "look good."

Rate Yourself on Using Negotiating Strategies and Tactics

How effective are you in using strategies and tactics in your sales negotiations?

- Using your own negotiating strengths and weaknesses to best advantage.
- Using the buyer's strengths and weaknesses to best advantage.
- Understanding clearly why the buyer is negotiating with you.
- Thinking-through what your concession curve should look like.
- Understanding the timing issues in each negotiation.
- Identifying all the key players.
- Thinking-through the best place to negotiate.
- Starting with high and convincing opening demands.
- Avoiding concessions by pleading lack of authority.
- Striving for more information to sidestep a concession.
- Using a "tough guy" to put pressure on the buyers.
- Using inexpensive changes as appealing concessions.
- Raising net profit with some little extras at the end.
- Sidestepping buyer demands with diversionary information.

- Changing the pace by switching negotiators.
- Using patience and temporary deadlocks.
- Building the buyer's ego.
- Thinking through some counter-tactics.

6

OPENING
THE NEGOTIATION

Sales Rep:	"Thanks for the coffee, Sal. Here's what I have. We can offer you the same service contract as last year at $550 a month."
(Note:	The sales rep can go as low as $500 if necessary.)
Customer:	"550! It was only $450 last year!"
Sales Rep:	"Yes, but we have all new equipment which will result in faster service calls—speed things up for you."
Customer:	"Don't expect me to pay for your new equipment. I'll pay $475, and that's it."
Sales Rep:	"Sal, we don't expect you to pay for our new equipment. But, we are going to be speeding up your service and cause less disruption to your operation."
(Note:	Both sides hang tough for the text 15 minutes.)
Customer:	"If I have to go to $500, I'll go that far. But then I want you here on Friday afternoon instead of whenever you find it convenient."
Sales Rep:	"Sal, I just can't go to $500. In fact, if you want us Friday afternoon I'll have to stay at $550. But I can agree to Friday afternoon at $550. (pause) Or, I can go to $540 for either Friday morning or Monday afternoon."
Customer:	"You're tough, you're tough. Okay, $540 for Friday morning."

OPENING PROPOSALS AND DEMANDS

We negotiate in practically every aspect of our lives. We negotiate priorities with our bosses, peers, and subordinates as well as with our families and friends. We negotiate when we buy a car, present a proposal, hire a consultant, or move an office.

In Chapter 1, the face-to-face skills required of an effective sales negotiator were outlined. The very first of those addressed the initial stage of the "live" negotiation—the skill of presenting the opening demands and/or dealing with the opening offer presented by the other side.

In many ways this opening stage of offers and demands can be the most critical in terms of the message you send to your buyers. Right from the start you begin to communicate your firmness and the level of your expectations. And this is when you can make the first psychological dent in the buyer's own expectations. Since this can be so critical, and since you will frequently be pitted against skilled negotiators on the other side, the preparation and the psychological discipline, and the resolve with which you walk into that beginning stage, will begin to immediately pay benefits.

The primary hazard to avoid right off the bat is to unwittingly let anything reduce your targets and your expectations, which is the very first thing a skilled buyer will try to do. The other half of that hazard is for anybody on your negotiating team to say or do anything which will tend to encourage the other side to stick with their original targets and expectations.

How to Open High

It's been said before, but it is so important we'll repeat it—open high! Open as high as you think you can without destroying your credibility—and that may be a lot higher than some of your team members are ordinarily accustomed to thinking. "After all, if we have had a good working relationship with the other side for these many months or years, we don't want them to think we are suddenly becoming unreasonable." And that is precisely the kind of mushy thinking that can creep in ever so gently to lower your expectations during the opening handshakes and pleasantries.

For instance, what happens to your expectations when the other guys open by saying, "Jean, because of some difficulties that have cropped up recently in our plant we are not going to be able to talk with you about the full range of equipment we originally had in mind. We thought we might take a look at a scaled down set of possibilities." If you immediately start thinking, "How can we best scale this down and still make a profit?", when what your buyers really intended was simply to lower your expectations —i.e., to get basically the same package originally proposed but at a lower price —then they've *gotcha*. Do not let initial statements of gloom and doom trap you into untested assumptions, assumptions which lower your targets and expectations.

Conversely—if you begin "Sam, we've put a great deal of work into our proposal to hold the costs to the minimum, but we've recently been hit with a related price increase, so what we have to present to you today, of necessity, reflects those new price increases"—what do you suppose happens to his expectations?

Recognizing You Have a Lot of Strengths

One of the things you have done in your planning and preparation stage of the negotiation has been to make a list of your bargaining strengths. Now it's time to employ them. Use all the persuasion skills you would in a routine sales call. Combine that with a skillful determination to achieve the best results (e.g., net profit, long-term commitment, etc.) for your organization. In a give-and-take exchange you are now face-to-face with the buyer or contracting organization. A number of things are churning through your mind including questions, doubts, and your opponents' bargaining advantages. Well for goodness sake don't forget to churn your own strengths through there as well—it will strengthen your resolve. "We absolutely have to get this contract sewed up—but, wait a minute—they have to too." Or, "If they choose to get tough with us on the delivery dates they can really put some pressure on us—but, hold on now—we heard from one of their technical people that they consider our quality substantially higher than any competitor's." Or, "I know they're going to cry poor-mouth— then again, they think we are also negotiating with one of their competitors." Or, "If we don't make this sale we are really in trouble—of course, they need us as a back-up source, and they don't want to see us get into a jam."

You can always find a lot of things you have going for you if you set your mind to it. The critical thing is that the first few moments you walk into that bargaining session your attitude, your mental set, and your frame of mind must be focussed on how to capitalize on your strengths. Talk them through with your technical person in the car, the reception area, or the conference room just before you meet the other side face-to-face. Be sure you are not slipping into a cap-in-hand mood just because you want very badly to get a commitment. Even when you are by all counts in a very weak bargaining position resolve to parlay what minor strengths you can muster into a few extra percentage points in your favor. Rather than weakly conceding those few points to the other side, you can make a surprising difference in the bottom line net by concentrating on your strengths.

Positioning Your Proposal and Your Demands

Following is a list of 12 points to remember as you make your opening proposal to the prospective buyer, or contracting party, with whom you are about to negotiate:

1. Open *high*. Yes, we've said it again.
2. Substantiate your opening proposal with rationale.
3. Mention your awareness of their needs and requirements.
4. Unless you are trying for a win-lose, convey a problem-solving mood rather than obstinance.
5. Boost their ego. Even in the heat of disagreement never puncture their ego.
6. Do not offer a detailed cost breakdown. To have opened high you will have included a lot of cushion.
7. Give yourself elbow-room to make some concessions. Don't give anything away until you need to, even if it's insignificant to your side. You may need it later to draw out a concession you want from them.
8. Set the pace, both in terms of climate and resolve.
9. Convey a firm and decisive posture, but with understanding of their position.
10. In your remarks do not convey notions of concessions you may offer later by any acknowledgement of their strengths or your weaknesses.
11. Keep at least a mental list of any clues they convey in their initial reactions to your opening proposal.
12. If the other side opens first, avoid lowering the demands in your initial proposal.

New information may well be introduced early on in the bargaining which could prompt you to lower your sights. Do not fall into a trap. Through patient questioning test the validity and applicability of any new data and the assumptions involved before you leap to a lower level of expectations. Oftentimes you will enter into a negotiation fully aware of some areas of information you need to gather or to clarify during the bargaining. Hence, your proposal will have some tentative aspects. There is a world of difference in presenting these aspects— i.e., data gaps—in a factual information gathering mode as opposed to giving the appearance of a weak or shaky and poorly thought out proposal.

Dealing with the Opposing Offer and Counter-Offer

The effective sales negotiator must be able to react appropriately to the offers and demands, frequently unanticipated, by the other side. Despite the finest planning and preparation you don't really know what you will be confronted with until the bargaining begins. Following is a list of the dozen most frequent situations most likely to require your effective reaction in dealing with your buyer's opening offer or opening counter-offer:

- *Their opening offer is much lower than you had anticipated.* For example, they begin with, "We have assessed the property and have done a pretty thorough analysis. We have concluded that we cannot consider a price in excess of $260,000." Now how will you respond to that when your planned asking price was to be $420,000? Well, you will respond with $420,000, of course. Presumably you have prepared a reasonable rationale for your price and you are not about to make that first big concession. You will not make that first big concession!

- *The Manager of Purchasing of a valued account responds emotionally to your opening proposal.* In a quivering anger he roars, "We have been doing business with you people for 12 years, and now you pull this garbage on us—a 10% price hike; you must be crazy to think we'd go along with something like that!" Patience, patience. This will take time. Remember, if he's a purchasing executive he's probably a skilled negotiator, so don't lower sights yet. Show some understanding like, "Yes, Ralph, you have been a valued customer for quite awhile." Then wait, and let him blow off some more steam. But don't even begin to think about lowering your targets at this early point.

- *One of your own team members is impulsive and not too astute, but is needed for his technical expertise.* Your buyers open something like this: "We have studied your proposal and we feel that Mechanism B is an unnecessary add-on to the system. We wish to drop it and reduce the price by $45,000." The fact is that Mechanism B is going to save both you and the buyer untold man-days of aggravation because it's a backup subsystem and its inclusion has enabled you to reduce costs on the primary systems. But your good old technical wizard jumps in with, "Technically we should have no problem eliminating it." Who needs negotiating opponents with team members like this? The last thing you need at this point is to have to explain the cost reductions you realized on the primary systems. And you certainly do not want an internal negotiation, even bickering, within your own team. Your team members must be under control at the starting gun or an impulsive comment can blow the whole negotiation right at the opening offer.

• *Their opening counter-offer puts some heavy pressure on you.* "Gentlemen, we have looked at two other proposals and frankly yours is the weakest of the three. We need to wrap this up by tomorrow, so unless you can reduce your quote considerably I'm afraid we'll have to exclude you from consideration." Do not lower your expectations in a state of panic. Begin probing for non-cost-related information. Only after you have gathered more information can you assess their firmness and their tenacity. Your goal is still to maneuver them into making the first concession. To do that you need to let them offer a nugget of rationale that will permit them to make an initial concession without losing face.

• *Their opening offer is based on old assumptions.* For example, a company with whom you have contracted services for several years may well base their contract assumptions on precedent. If you permit them to do that you may get caught in an unexpected bind, because writing a contract based on precedent does not allow for unexpected future cost increases to you, changes in the law, environmental problems, sudden supply shortages, and many other factors which you should consider when you prepare a sales contract or a contract renewal.

• *Negotiating traps in opening offers.* Beware of that prospective buyer who seems just too sweet to be true as he makes his opening offer. A clever negotiating buyer could just love you right into the red ink column. That is not to suggest that all nice people are suspect, but in negotiations it can be—we say "can be"—a ploy.

• *They open with a take-it-or-leave-it.* Like, "Fellows, we'll give you 31 cents a pound and that's it." You really need 33 cents, and in fact your opening demand was 36 cents. If your planning was done properly you already know whether or not you are willing to get into a deadlock situation with these people, and walk out without an agreement, at least for the time being. But even if you are willing to do that your need is to get them make the first concession, and the sooner the better. So don't walk out just yet. Work on them for a bit, because time is valuable, and maybe you can help them find a way to gracefully make that first significant concession. To make it easier for them to do this you need to give them some rationale for your 33 (or more)-cent price. Remember, if they do concede they need to be prepared to give their management some darned good reasons why, and you are the one who must equip them with the reasons. In addition to such rationale, it's important to have some minor concessions in hand to offer them as well, once they have granted you the major one.

- *You sense that they have sent you the wrong negotiator.* For instance, you walk in and are met by a third-level subordinate who says, "Tom and Betty are tied up today so they asked me to sit in for them." This can be touchy. Even if he is not the key person you feel you should be bargaining with, you need to be very careful not to offend him. He may not have the authority to make an opening offer or counter-offer. He may not have sufficient knowledge. Or, maybe he has been sent in to gather as much information as possible to feed back to the real negotiators giving them more time and substance for preparation. He may be an obstinate type who is simply there to soften you up. Whatever the reason is, treat him with respect. Gather as much information as he will convey. And don't give away any more than you need to, including the opening demand, if you judge he is not in position to bargain.

- *They hit you with a rush deadline.* This can be hazardous, so first try to determine, through some (who, what, when, where, why, and how) questioning, whether they are under real pressure or is it a ploy to get a commitment from you before you have all the facts. This is especially critical if there is a wide gap between your opening proposal and their opening offer. On the one hand you need to avoid taking advantage of a respected long-range relationship while protecting your own interests against hasty errors. The key to accomplishing this is your ability to effectively gather and assess critical information under time pressure.

- *They snow a mass of data upon you.* Your potential buyers bring a bevy of accountants and technical experts who propose a complex formula in their opening offer which is supported by mounds of documentation. Time out! The bargaining table is no place to try to analyze complex data. This is clearly a time for adjournment, caucus, and resourcing of your own experts.

- *Their approach is downright obnoxious.* Again, is it a ploy, is this a win-lose, or are they just naturally offensive? Don't cut off your nose to spite your face. Patience, information gathering, and tenacity are the keys in dealing with these types.

- *They advise you there will be a delay.* Quite a normal thing to happen, but don't let it subtly lower your expectation level. Do not automatically offer some concessions, "to speed things up," until you are certain things can be sped up. After all, the delay may be very legitimate and totally unrelated to your proposal. On the other hand, it could be a conscious delaying tactic. If you made the opening offer, and let slip that you are under pressure to reach an agreement, your buyers, if they are at all skilled, are apt to employ the old delaying tactic in order to draw some concessions from you. Thus, the messages you send in that opening are critical in revealing or not, to the other side, what tactics they may be able to employ against you, particularly in terms of time pressure tactics. The same works in reverse. Be alert in their opening offer or counter-offer to any strengths you can pick up, any weaknesses they convey, and the related tactics you might employ.

The opening offers and counter-offers are critical to the negotiation, not just in terms of their quantitative levels (prices, conditions, and the like), but in terms of the hidden messages the two sides communicate in those vital opening exchanges. The climate, the resolve, the apparent skill or lack thereof, and the preparation done is all communicated in some degree during those opening offers and counter-offers. It is a critical time to guard against slippage in your own levels of expectations. It is the time when your prospective buyer or contracting party will be hitting you with their very worst offer, bleakest of information. Be ready to absorb the shocks, to give and take, and to maneuver the results in your favor throughout the bargaining to follow.

12-Point Checklist for Opening a Negotiation

1. Open high.
2. Give reasons for your high demands.
3. Acknowledge the buyer's needs.
4. Convey a problem-solving mood.
5. Boost the buyer's ego.
6. Do not give cost details.
7. Don't make a concession until you need to.
8. Set the pace.
9. Be decisive, but with understanding.
10. Do not focus on your weaknesses or the buyer's strengths.
11. Mentally note the buyer's early signals.
12. If the buyer opens first, do not lower your expectations.

Sales Rep:	"Mrs. James, I'm not sure we have a totally clear picture about your packaging requirements. Could you fill me in a little more?"
Mrs. James:	"Our material is highly sensitive to contamination from minute debris in packaging materials. We can't have that."
Sales Rep:	"Is that why you're specifying glass liners in our containers?"

Rate Yourself on Your Skills at Opening a Negotiation

How effective are you at starting a sales negotiation off on the right foot?

- Sending signals of strength in your opening remarks.
- Maintaining high targets when the buyer opens strong.
- Focusing on your strengths under pressure.
- Giving reasons for your high demands.
- Boosting the buyer's ego early-on.
- Responding effectively to early surprises.
- Dealing with emotional buyers.
- Coaching any support people what to avoid.
- Detecting invalid assumptions.
- Fending off ploys that are too sweet to be true.
- Dealing with substitutes who have no authority.
- Responding to tough opening tactics from buyers.
- Separating legitimate delays from tactical delays.
- Deferring reaction to buyers' opening tactics.

Mrs. James:	"Absolutely." (Long pause...silence) "We know it's more expensive, but contamination is our number one concern."
Sales Rep:	"How important is cost?"
Mrs. James:	"Naturally cost is important. Especially because of our expensive packaging specifications. It really pinches our margins. But we have to have glass liners to prevent contamination in the raw materials we buy from you."
Sales Rep:	"If we could provide a less expensive liner that passes your own lab tests, would you give us an additional 20% of your orders?"

(Long pause...silence)

Mrs. James:	"Maybe some, not 20%"
Sales Rep:	"We've come across a new high-grade polyethylene liner. We could save you 4 cents a container. But we couldn't justify our conversion costs without about a 20% volume increase."
Mrs. James:	"If you can save us 7 cents you're on."
Sales Rep:	"Seven cents is a lot. Could you go 5 cents?" (Long pause)
Mrs. James:	"Okay, 5 cents; that's acceptable."

GATHERING INFORMATION FACE-TO-FACE

In spite of all the best planning in the world a great deal of the information you need with which to negotiate effectively, must be gathered during the face-to-face discussions. In most cases you cannot assemble in advance everything you need to know about the buyer's objectives, constraints, strengths, weaknesses, strategies, tactics, and product or service details. Furthermore, some of the information you put together in advance will be inaccurate, incomplete, or will have changed by negotiating time. In fact, part of your advance planning must include those questions and tactics you will be using during the live bargaining to gather more useable information. Thus, a great deal of the face-to-face negotiating time is actually nothing more than gathering and mentally processing useable information.

In larger negotiations involving major long-range commitments, the first few meetings may be totally dedicated to information gathering. In these cases a blitz-team approach may be used to gather and assemble a great deal of information during the initial meetings. Each team member has an assigned area of information for which he or she is responsible, including such intelligence as the buyer's probable objectives, strategies, strengths, and weaknesses.

In other team-type negotiations, one team member may be as-signed the sole task of taking notes and recording information on everything from body language to technical detail. The advantage in this approach is that you can devote your total attention to picking up facts and clues without the need to be constantly reacting to questions and tactics employed by the other side. You can signal your team leader to caucus when you see the need or an opportunity, but may otherwise stay completely out of the give-and-take discussion.

Key Kinds of Information to Be Gathered Live

One thing you need to know about that buyer or contractor across the table is "does he have any kind of 'hidden agenda' in this negotia-tion that may vitally affect his ability or willingness to give and take?" By hidden agenda we mean issues which are not directly related to the pure business rationale of the negotiation but which are affecting his attitude or his willingness to deal with you on a strictly business basis. The most common examples of this would be:

   a. Personal matters, like his boss has given him a poor rating on his annual review.
   b. Internal politics, such as an executive in his organization who hates an executive in your organization.
   c. Strategic ploys, perhaps to mislead you about their needs or intentions.

These kinds of hidden agenda issues can involve a whole new dimension of "their" objectives which are just as critical to the results of the negotiation as any of the rational business-related objectives. It is vital that the effective sales negotiator pick up any clues the buyer or potential customer may be communicating indirectly that could reveal hidden agenda objectives.

The most common kind of information-gathering function of the live bargaining is simply obtaining any new information that the other side is willing to share with you; that is, new information directly related to the key issues of the negotiation. Additional facts and ideas about pricing, specifications, schedules, and the like will probably be shared in more depth, offering better insight during the face-to-face process than you've been able to gain in writing or by telephone. Know what additional data you want to gather face-to-face, but be alert for new items you had not anticipated as they are revealed during the discussion. And most importantly, maintain the flexibility to adjust your strategies and tactics as warranted by new facts and insights. This is one reason why a sales negotiator needs the ability to think quickly under stress in order to effectively process and use new information that comes out during the process of give-and-take.

Another key area in which to gather additional facts and insights face-to-face involves the nature of the alternatives (to your offer or proposal) the prospective buyer is considering. Who are the competitors, if any? What noncompetitor-related alternatives are there? What are the real strengths and weaknesses of each, including the do-not-buy-now alternative.

One way of looking at the face-to-face information gathering process is in terms of your original Negotiation Planning Sheet (see Chapter 2). What gaps need to be filled-in? What updating is needed? What new areas of information do you need to explore?

Eight Rules for Gathering Negotiating Intelligence Face-to-Face

Patience is fundamental to each of the following; even when you are employing emotionalism as a tactic, patience is fundamental:

1. *Keep Quiet and Listen.* Effective listening is sort of a two-part skill. First of all you need to discipline yourself to keep quiet. This can be very difficult during long periods of silence, but let the other guy break the silence. You'll learn more about him that way. The second part of the listening skill involves mentally recording and processing what you hear. This takes effort but if you don't mentally record it and process it, then why listen?

2. *No Quick Commitments.* Whether in person or by telephone, don't agree to anything without asking yourself, "Do I need to think about this for a minute?" What's the rush? Do you really need to make a commitment this very instant? How about, "Let me think about it, and I'll get back to you on that." You may just discover you need more information before you make that commitment.

3. *Test the Assumptions.* Remember that in the planning stage of the negotiation you listed the assumptions that need testing. Well, now is the time to test them. For instance, "Mrs. Buyer, could you tell us a little about the relative importance of this set of specifications?" Or, "Mr. Builder, why do you feel the local zoning laws can't be modified during the next year or so?"

4. *Using Resistance Techniques.* Use them for the purpose of drawing out more information. "We'd love to, but .." is an excellent technique for getting the prospect to either verify his resolve or respond with suggested alternative ways you might help him, and which may give you vital information about his real needs. "We'd love to make that

modification for you, but it would probably delay your startup by three months," could draw out all sorts of information from him on everything from timing pressures to price flexibility

Another useful resistance-type technique you can employ strictly for the purpose of drawing out more information is to respond to a request from the buyer by simply terminating the discussion. For example, "I'm afraid this is a firm price, Mr. Customer, so give it some consideration and I'll get back to you next week to see if we can go forward on it." If you can afford to take this position, the customer may well offer some information which will help you to make a minor concession which will lead to a commitment. Another example might be, "Well, I'll have to study your counter-proposal and get back to you." Again, when he sees you walking out he may offer some further information which tends to modify the counter-proposal and related demands. In a team negotiation, just getting up to caucus can sometimes draw additional information from the other side if they have cause to be anxious about the results of the caucus. Using techniques for temporarily interrupting the face-to-face bargaining certainly has limited application but it can be a useful way of drawing out additional ideas, counter-proposals, and hints for concessions from the other side. The most opportune time to employ this type of technique is when you feel that there is more information the other side can and will give you, and when they are under some motivation to move the negotiation along toward a successful conclusion.

An additional resistance technique sales negotiators often use to stimulate prospective buyers into sharing more data is to advise them that since you (the sales negotiator) "would have to clear any modification request with higher authority, you will need some additional background information to support such a request." Faced with this new alternative, the prospect may withdraw his request if he was only testing your resolve—or, he may indeed offer some cost or benefit information. This will enable you to ask for a concession in return, or even satisfy his request with a lesser concession. "Well, based on that, Mr. Prospect, we can no doubt delay invoicing until January 2, but from what you describe you don't actually need delivery until December 15 anyway."

5. *Try Some Effective Questioning.* Now you may be asking, "Why wasn't this listed first, since it's the most obvious way of gathering information in a negotiation?" You're right. It clearly is, but some of the less obvious rules needed consideration before we get to this more apparent one. Let's look at some different kinds of questioning techniques to be used in a sales negotiation.

The first kind of question to use is one that encourages the other party to respond with a great deal of information. For example, "Mr.

A, before we try to respond to your price reduction proposal, I wonder if you could tell us a little more about your planned process applications; you know, your scheduling, expected volumes, and the like?" Provided you have left him some elbow room—i.e., you've not pressed him for any sensitive information—he is quite apt to tell you an awful lot that could help you to seek some counter-concessions on everything from specifications to delivery flexibility. By asking broad questions that relate to his product or market, or whatever is relevant to the negotiation at hand, rather than a specific question requiring a very short answer, you are encouraging him to open up and provide you with opportunities for give-and-take. Another example, "What kinds of efficiencies are you expecting with this new concept, Mr. Buyer?"

If after attempting this broad questioning approach there are still some specific pieces of information you need, then you may simply ask some direct questions: "Mrs. B. have you looked at Brand "x" copiers yet?", "What are you paying per gross now?", "Would you be willing to tell us what percent of your business we are currently getting?" Sometimes direct questions are the only way to get some of the data you need, despite the risk you take in having the other person decline sharing certain data with you.

If that happens you may need to take an indirect approach in getting at certain key data. For example, a sales negotiator often resorts to casual conversation about a seemingly unrelated aspect of the customer's business. You might even converse with another employee of the organization (e.g., a technical person, a line supervisor, etc.) to draw out some critical piece of information about a competitor, long-range plans, or some other vital intelligence. This indirect approach to questioning can be particularly effective in a casual setting, over lunch or cocktails, or after the formal discussions.

Another technique of drawing out information closely related to questioning is the use of the misstatement-of-fact: "Jack, I understand you people feel you can increase your productivity by over 15% by using our facilities," when you only have a hint, or suspicion, or approximation of information to that effect. Risky or not, this approach is often used in hopes of eliciting some more exacting data from the other side.

One final method of questioning is the redirected question. Example: A prospective buyer throws a question at you about the expected cost savings he should realize with your new system. You redirect the question to one of his associates, or even back to him. Refer to some prior savings opportunities they had revealed, inviting them to elaborate in more depth. Here again, you use this technique for the purpose of additional information gathering.

6. *Using the "If-We-Do-This Technique."* When key issues get a bit sticky and things are at an impasse you need a tool to bring the process off dead-

center. One critical element in accomplishing this is new or reposi-tioned information. A very good tool for placing things in a new perspective to elicit new information is to pose some alternative twists to those key issues. For example, "What if we could deliver this order in three separate segments over the first quarter of next year, Mr. Buyer?" Mr. Buyer almost has to respond with some kind of informa-tion about his operation as to why or why not that approach would be useful. An effective sales negotiator will think of all sorts of what-if kinds of alternatives to draw out new information when the bargaining seems to be at a complete standstill.

7. *Reach an Intentional Deadlock.* This is closely related to the resistance technique, but more definite. If time and bargaining strength is on your side, and the other party will not engage in adequate give-and-take exchange of information, courteously state your deadlocked position and leave. If later, they decide to share some information which can generate a mutual give-and-take, the negotiation can be resumed.

8. *Remember, They Are Gathering Information Too.* It bears repeating. Do not blunder into giving unnecessary information to the buyer or prospect. Excess information may become ammunition in his arsenal for lowering your aspiration levels later on. There is a fine line here between cooperative bargaining with a trusted long-term account and blurting out unnecessary tidbits. That fine line does require conscious and rational consideration. Even in a Lose-Win negotiation, where you may be asking a faithful business partner to bail you out of a bind, you still need to draw the line between information he needs in order to help you, and that which is not necessary to share with him to meet your objectives.

A skilled buyer may attempt any of the following techniques to psych you into giving him confidential-type information:

a. Requesting estimates in advance, before you really have time to think them through: He will be able to squeeze information from you later on by holding you to your initial estimates of cost, time, specification tolerances, etc.

b. Suggesting you're not quite close enough: If you respond by giving him detailed rationale for your proposal you may be giving him information which he can use to pull other concessions from you. The degree of "detail" is the issue here.

c. Asking for cost details: Guaranteed, if you share detailed costs he will find some soft spots or areas of cushion to seek additional concessions. A skilled buyer will usually attempt this one. Be prepared for it.

d. Giving misleading competitive data: To draw more data from you, some buyers will use this technique, ethical or not.

One final information-gathering technique which you may employ, or may have employed against you, is that of going "off the record." More useable bargaining information is inadvertently, and at times by design, shared over cocktails, coffee, or lunch, than may ever be shared in the formal negotiating atmosphere of the office or the conference room.

In entering any sales negotiation, you need to keep two cautions in mind. However thorough you believe your planning and preparation has been, caution number one, "Do not fall in love with your plan." It will be incomplete. It may even be inaccurate. Be prepared to take your time to test it out, and fill in the gaps with some patient information gathering once you meet your buyers face-to-face.

Caution number two is, "Do not blurt out information to the buyer, information you will later regret." Skillful buyers may pressure you, or bait you, into revealing information which will weaken your negotiating position and strengthen theirs. Again, this may sound like win-lose strategy. But since there is rarely a pure win-win, or pure win-lose, caution is always appropriate.

The gathering and protecting of information during the face-to-face encounter is one of the critical issues in effective sales negotiations.

**Face-to-Face
Information Gathering Worksheet**

Following are the question categories you may use to fill in your
information voids regarding the buyers':

. . . .

NEGOTIATION OBJECTIVES

PERSONAL CONCERNS

ORGANIZATIONAL ISSUES

ASSUMPTIONS

RISKS

ALTERNATIVES

Rate Yourself on Face-to-Face Information Gathering Skills

How effective are you at gathering critical information during the face-to-face negotiation?

- Recognizing that your prenegotiation information is incomplete and often inaccurate.

- Sensing a hidden agenda.

- Sticking with a probing, questioning approach under stress.

- Keeping quiet and listening.

- Withholding quick responses.

- Testing assumptions.

- Using resistance techniques.

- Asking broad questions to encourage a lot of information.

- Asking specific follow-through questions to zero-in.

- Using indirect questioning and probing techniques.

- Using the "if-we-do-this" technique.

- Using intentional deadlocks to force out more information.

- Resisting release of unnecessary information to the buyer.

7

ESTABLISHING CREDIBILITY

Buyer:	"It seems to me your proposal includes a gross overkill in safety gear. I mean, we're all for safety, but this is a bit much."
Sales Rep:	"Our company policy is to adhere strictly with industry safety standards."
Buyer:	"Well, it looks to me as though you are over-complying, and building some fat into your proposal."
Seller:	"The only difference between this and your Murray Hill contract is the item on sleeves. And if the bill pending in the state legislature passes, as we expect, you'd be forced to add them later at an even greater expense."
Buyer:	"Maybe, but you've got a lot of items in there I doubt we really need for safety compliance."
Seller:	"I have here a printed summary of the relevant safety regulations, including those pending, for each state in the four-state area. Here, you may keep this copy."
Buyer:	"Okay, but I still think you're asking us to pay through the nose for all this."
Seller:	"Here. Let me show you some slides we've brought along. They show statistically the long-term savings in lost time, insurance costs, and litigation costs based on a ten-year study."

(20 minutes later.)

Buyer:	"May I borrow some of this to show my management?"

ESTABLISHING CREDIBILITY

One of the most critical aspects of success in a sales negotiation is the other party's perception of both you and your proposal in terms of credibility. The prospective buyer or account must believe that you and your organization are people with whom he can benefit by conducting the negotiation. He must also believe that your proposal is realistic and of value.

Time and again throughout the negotiation he may test the credibility of specific issues in your proposal, thus you must be prepared to defend each specific point, not just the proposal in general. This may sound too obvious for comment, but time after time sales negotiators get trapped by skilled purchasing professionals who are probing for credibility gaps in each specific part of the proposal.

Credibility is, of course, a two-way street. It's the other guy's responsibility to pick holes in the validity of your proposal details in order to get concessions from you.

On the other side of the coin is the reasonableness and the value to you of the buyer's request or offer or counter-proposal. A clever prospect may try to lead you to believe that he has already shopped around your various competition. Too often the sales negotiator fails to test the depth of knowledge the prospect has gained by his purported shopping around. Although the ideas discussed in this chapter are presented as tools to be used by the sales negotiator, the effective buyer is using a similar set of tools in attempting to establish with you the credibility of his requests and offers.

As suggested above, negotiating credibility is divided into two parts: first, the personal credibility of the individuals involved in the negotiation, and second, the credibility of the issues in the proposal, or offer, and counter-proposals. Personal credibility issues include knowledge, authority, confidence, and intent, such as the willingness to give and take. Credibility issues involving the proposal include the validity of price information, performance claims, and the like.

Demonstrating Personal Credibility

"Mr. Prospect, I don't have the authority to discuss price with you and I don't really know much about the specifications of this stuff, but the front office insisted that I get a general idea from you about your interests in our proposal—and, by the way, this is our first attempt to produce this kind of thing." Here I'm just trying to demonstrate in one paragraph what often takes the wrong negotiator a half a day to say.

Or, how about, "Jim, I've brought along Hank here from our advertising staff to explain our technical superiority, and Sandy over here from the scientific research group to give you a good feel for our accounting procedures, and Smith here will be your Account Manager, after he finishes his training program." A bit overstated maybe, but do you think these kinds of things don't really happen?

Demonstrating the Credibility of Your Proposal

What kinds of things in your sales proposal might a prospective buyer question, in terms of credibility? Well, first of all he will probably wonder if your price is fair and realistic.

Assuming the price package appears to be within a realistic negotiating range, the next credibility test (understand, these do not necessarily fall in any particular sequence) the prospect will consider is the product or service qualities and benefits the sales negotiator has presented. "This old plant has been in operation for 30 years. Maybe these guys are giving us a line about the true operating costs we'd experience if we were to undertake a long-term lease." Whether you are trying to sell a lease on an old plant facility or on a new software package, the prospect has some credibility type questions he will use to whittle down your price aspiration level. A prompt, firm, and rational response to each credibility issue raised by your potential buyer is the surest way to shift the bargaining in your side's favor.

Another big gray area of credibility issues in the prospect's mind is, "Can these guys really deliver? Can they give us as much as we need, when we need it, according to all our specs, without significant cost overruns and time delays."

In addition to these basic areas of credibility issues there are others: legal compliance, human and labor relations concerns, administrative convenience, and long-term impact. Any of these may pop up unexpectedly at some point during the negotiations and must be dealt with effectively at the time or the credibility of the entire sales proposal will erode.

Seven Tools for Establishing Credibility

Each of the following tools may be used by or against the negotiator of a sales proposal:

1. *Industry Standard.* "Well Sir, that's the standard discount policy in this product line and we are obligated to adhere to that." Or, "Yes, this is the standard warranty offered for rebuilt equipment according to the trade association standards." How about, "Well, these are the published conference packaging requirements which we are committed to." Or "We can certainly find some way to work this out to your satisfaction, but the 7% commission is the required level by Realtors in this state." Or finally, "I wish we could get this industry regulation amended, but for now we are obligated to apply this surcharge."

Each of the issues relevant to the above "credibility" responses by the sales negotiator is probably negotiable. Remember, oftentimes the buyer with whom you are bargaining simply needs some rationale to take back to his organization to justify the price to which he has agreed. If standard industry practice is an acceptable rationale for him, then by all means use it!

2. *Facts and Statistics.* The book *How to Lie with Statistics*, By Darrell Huff, describes some delightfully clever ways that all of us can be deceived by statistical presentation. Lying is not condonable, but the problem is that deception comes in many shades of gray.

It is the salesperson's responsibility to test the validity and applicability of any facts or statistics the buying organization presents, and vice versa. That is not to suggest a philosophy of let the buyer beware, but the point is you must equip yourself with any factual support materials available which may give credibility to the sales proposal in the eyes of the prospective buyer. And since you cannot always predict what kinds of data will impress a prospect, it is the prospect's responsibility to test the pertinence of whatever is presented to him. If a prospective buyer is not quantitatively oriented, he may be very easily "snowed" by some graphs, charts, and other presentations which are only indirectly related to the key issues. Of course a skeptical buyer may need statistical overkill just to get him to move at all.

"Mr. Adams, I have here a series of charts, with supporting data, which give you the ten-year history of the key indicators we have described." You had this compiled in response to Adams' two-year study which reflected a less than typical short-term turndown in two of the key indicators in question. Or, for example, your account shows you an exhibit which indicates a net loss for the past year on using your product, while at the same time her forecast for the next three years (which she isn't showing you) suggests a handsome profit. Your facts and data must be sufficiently comprehensive and complete to put her limited picture into perspective. This can be accomplished without causing her to lose face and may just give her the ammunition she needs to get the commitment you need from her superiors.

The effective sales negotiator carries with him more facts and statistical support, including team member specialists, than he will probably need. But the prospective buyer may do the very same thing. The sales side must test the data presented by the buyer's side. Does the data cover a valid time period? Does it include a sufficient sampling to support the buyer's conclusions? Are the specialists and experts there just for effect. Are they attempting to snow you with irrelevant data and do you need to back-off and refer their data to your own experts? These are questions the sales negotiating team needs to deal with on the spot, react effectively to, and call a caucus about if appropriate.

3. *Using Media for Credibility.* "Mr. Prospect, before we meet next Friday to conclude the agreement, I have an article here from the *Neolithic Journal* I thought you might like to read. It goes into some depth in describing the future demand for post-Paleolithic derivatives and some of the innovative research our people have been doing in this area." An article from an industry journal, or from a prestigious general business periodical, about your product, service, or people can make a significant plus in the mind of your prospect. Any sort of media from respected sources such as satisfied accounts, highly regarded independent research organizations, as well as internally designed presentations, should be used by your team during the negotiation. Specifically target your timing as to where each piece is introduced for credibility purposes as needed during the bargaining. If a negotiation involves several meetings, the negotiating strategy needs to be updated after each session. Bring along the kinds of credibility support media next time to meet the needs of the particular individuals on the opposing team.

Will there be an accountant or an engineer? What kinds of media will impress them as credible? Will a graphic slide presentation give an air of professionalism? Should videotape or film or flip-charts be considered? There are dozens of kinds and combinations of media to be considered for the purposes of conveying credibility, mostly in terms of professionalism. But the key is to match the right media to the specific individuals on the opposing team.

4. *Printed Documents and Labels.* Let's say you have some excess capacity and you have made contact with a few prospective users of that capacity on a contract basis. We will assume that you are in a buyer's market, that there is similar excess capacity available elsewhere, and that your prospects are generally aware of this. Might it be useful to approach these prospects with a preprinted "standard contract" form with the terms and conditions all spelled out in advance?

Of course those terms and conditions are negotiable, but wouldn't it add an air of credibility to have them presented in a standard contract format? Whether it's excess capacity, excess product, or excess services available, a preprinted contract may just be a starting point for negotiation. It can provide the solid base of credibility with which to establish an interest by the prospect for a productive give-and-take.

Let's take another case—the standard price label. Do we ever see products which could carry a standard price label but don't? Especially in areas like used and refurnished equipment we see it every day. Just because we have some product we want to get rid of, or is of secondary importance to our sales efforts, that is no reason to forego the credibility value of placing a standard pricing label on it as a starting point for negotiation.

There is just something abut a preprinted form, contract, or price list that makes it look official, hence credible. Consider the groundskeeper who comes around to your company to peddle his services. What impression will he leave if he approaches your maintenance services manager with a standard contract form detailing his price per hour for lawn mowing, hedge trimming, and other services. This as compared to the weakened negotiating position he would leave himself in if he were to simply make his approach without any sort of document in hand.

Granted, most organizations have such standard pricing and specification documents for their basic product line or services. But how about all those ancillary or extra add-ons buyers request from you? Consider all those potentially high net profit (or straight-off-the-top costs) items which are so often offered as a service to your customer, but for which the customer may well be willing to pay, if only he were given a credible document to support your pricing. In that face-to-face meeting in a negotiation, much credibility can be gained with a strategy of preprinted "standard" price lists and contracts.

5. *Laws and Regulations.* As government bureaucracy grows we are harassed with more and more requirements and restrictions in our sales contracts. We always seem to look at this from the negative side but it behooves us to look for opportunities as well. Oftentimes laws and regulations can be used as credible reasons to deny expensive requests by buyers for special treatment.

The Sherman Act, for example, prohibits not only price fixing amongst competitors, but reciprocity between sellers and buyers. Hence, if a buyer offers a "deal" involving reciprocity in order to pull down your asking price, your credibility tool for declining may well be, "We'll need to check this out with our legal counsel regarding Sherman Act implications."

Even the Clayton Act, which restricts sellers from maneuvering buyers into exclusive arrangements, may be used as a credibility tool by a sales negotiator in responding to a prospective purchaser who offers an "exclusive" commitment as a bargaining weapon. There are numerous cases where exclusivity may be of no particular value to you as a seller. The account is too small to matter. You are phasing out of that particular market etc, etc. Again, if it appears that the purchaser is offering a meaningless exclusive buying arrangement simply to gain other concessions from you you may simply respond, "I'm, afraid I'll need to refer that to our legal department" (for Clayton Act implications).

A third classic law to be used as a credibility tool in warding off requests for concessions is the Robinson-Patman Act. Not only does Robinson-Patman prohibit price discrimination between purchasers of commodities of like grade and quality (where the effect would be to limit competition), but it also prohibits discriminatory merchandising assistance, certain discount systems and volume pricing arrangements, as well as some freight absorption deals between seller and buyer.

The intent here is not to suggest you attempt an interpretation of any of these laws as they might pertain to a given sales negotiation, but to alert you to some of the key issues and to the possibility of using them to establish credibility in defense of the proposal you are presenting to a prospective buyer. Referral to legal counsel is, of course, the proper route to take if the buyer doesn't withdraw his request or counter-proposal at first mention of these legal implications. There are, of course, many other legal and regulatory issues that apply to your particular industry. Make it a point to become familiar with them. For just to be able to say, "Mr. Purchaser, we certainly understand the reason for your particular request, but the FDA, EPA, TOSCA, ICC, The Justice Department, and local ordinance XY 285590327 prevents us from offering that concession," can be a powerful set of credibility tools to be used in fending off costly concession requests.

6. *Precedents.* "Mrs. Black, we have done some research on this type of an arrangement and the way we find it has been handled by ourselves, and a couple other vendors in three or four past contracts, has been as follows: - - - - - ." What can sound more credible than to refer to precedents? Instead of you needing to defend the rationale of new ideas, the purchaser now has to find reasons why the precedent shouldn't apply to her—i.e., she is on the defensive instead of you.

7. *Policies and Procedures.* "Seven percent discount is our standard policy Mrs. Farley. For anything above that I would need to get approval from the VP, and he's out of town for the next three weeks." Or, "These procedures take into account our production flow, distribution system, and computerized program so that if we changed that item it would involve procedural changes all the way back through the total system."

In Summary

Procedures, precedents, laws, preprinted documents, media presentations, statistics, or industry practice—any or all of these, if used selectively, can give the sales negotiator the credibility needed in the proposal to capture the genuine interest of a prospect or ward off demands for costly concessions. This is not to downplay the importance of referring the prospective purchaser directly to evidence of other successful agreements you have completed, whether with his competitors or other credible parties. But it is to emphasize a number of major areas of opportunity for injecting credible strength into the issues you are proposing.

The more credible your proposal is perceived by the prospect, the more credible you and your organization. And unless you are able to establish that credibility on both fronts early on in your face-to-face negotiating, all the tactics and maneuvers to follow may be for naught.

CREDIBILITY PLANNER

Category   **Specifics We'll Use in This Negotiation**

. . . .

Policies &
Procedures

Precedents

Laws

Preprinted
Documents

Media
Presentations

Statistics

Industry
Practice

Other

Rate Yourself
at Establishing Credibility

How effective are you at establishing credibility regarding you, your organization, and each element of your proposal?

- Establishing, in the mind of the buyer, that your proposal is realistic and of value to him.

- Demonstrating your personal credibility.

- Giving credible reasons for your high opening price demands.

- Eliminating any doubts about your organization's ability to deliver.

- Citing industry standards and practices to defend your proposal.

- Assembling statistics and factual data to support your demands.

- Using media presentation to enhance credibility.

- Preparing printed documents to convey credibility.

- Referring to laws and regulations to fend off certain buyer demands.

- Using precedents to demonstrate credibility of your demands.

- Citing policies and procedures to justify certain demands.

- Identifying credibility gaps in the buyer's demands and counter-proposals.

- Gracefully pursuing any credibility gaps in the buyer's proposals without bruising his ego or esteem.

8

HOW TO USE
NEGOTIATING TACTICS
WHEN YOU MEET
FACE-TO-FACE

Sales Rep:	"Sorry, I can't really lower the price. That would have to go through the product manager and the marketing director."
Buyer:	"Well, your price is too high."
Sales Rep:	"Let's talk to your engineering manager. Maybe we could make some changes to save you money overall."

(15 minutes later)

Sales Rep:	"Do you really need all six belts on this model or could you accept four belts if we could save you a lot of money?"
Engineering Manager:	"We can easily go for four if you install the next larger size."
Sales Rep:	"That's certainly doable. We'll take $100 off the price."
Buyer:	"That's not enough. We need $200 off."
Sales Rep:	"I understand your high quality standards. Could we take a short break while I make a phone call?"

(10 minutes later)

Sales Rep: "We can give you $112 off if two belts are regular size and two are the next larger size."

Engineering
Manager: "That's fine, that's fine."

Buyer
(muttering to himself): "Yes, that's fine"

Sales Rep: "And for backup, why don't you take an extra inventory of heavier belts? You'll always have them for emergencies."

USING NEGOTIATING TACTICS

In Chapter 6 several different areas of tactics planning were discussed: opening demands, authority levels, informational, tough guy, changing negotiators, time-related tactics, and ego-building.

Chapter 7 described seven tools for establishing credibility: industry practice, facts and statistics, media tools, preprinted documents, laws and regulations, precedents, and policies or procedures.

Keeping the critical area of "climate" in mind let us now take a look at a negotiating situation involving the application and synthesis of many of these tactics and credibility tools. Synthesis is the key word here, for it's the bringing together of all the tactics, tools, strategies, skills, and planning into effective application in a sales negotiation that generates the ultimate payoff. So let's consider now the case of Charlie Simpson who, with his engineering and production colleagues, has just completed a team negotiation with the Central Utilities Company of Pinetree City. Charlie was by himself in the initial meeting with Mr. Wattkins, the Central Utilities representative. Although he wanted to achieve a win-win result by the close of the negotiation, Charlie was not at all sure the Central people were going to be that reasonable to deal with.

Conducting the Initial Meeting

During that first meeting Charlie hit Mr. Wattkins with a price of $293,870 (his minimum acceptable price was $265,000) for a proposed package, including equipment and all auxiliary gear as spelled out in Central's initial request for quotation. Wattkins indicated that the price (which was 20% over Charlie's minimum acceptable price) was way above his expectation, and that he could never present such a costly proposal to his vice-president.

Charlie had presented a formal contract with all the details spelled out, for Wattkins' initialing of acceptance, even though the contract would require routine approval by Central's legal staff. However, when Wattkins resisted the price quotation as "at least $30,000 too high," Charlie began pressing for a major concession.

Wattkins did not respond with any concession other than to firm up a counter-offer of $260,000 after a couple of phone calls to somebody in his cost analysis group. So Charlie tactfully requested a meeting with the vice-president. He offered to bring somebody from his own Engineering Department to help describe the technical justification background in the proposal. At first Wattkins balked at this request, but Charlie was gently persistent so Wattkins finally agreed. Overall it looked like a pretty sound proposal and perhaps a session with the VP could shorten the negotiation by once and for all confirming that they (Central) were not about to pay that high a price for this contract. It was agreed that Wattkins would confirm such a meeting to Charlie sometime within the next week.

Before concluding their initial meeting, though, there was some additional fact-finding Charlie wanted to do so he could be fully prepared for the crucial bargaining with the VP. In the process of probing for insights about the VP's attitudes and priorities related to this contract, Charlie drew out some interesting facts from Wattkins. The VP was a tiger on engineering quality, and the reason Charlie's firm had been asked to quote was because of the VP's "respect for your engineering reputation." Charlie also learned that the VP was anxious to get the installation underway, apparently because some other expansion project was dependent on completion of this job. Wattkins also alluded to the fact that one other firm had been asked to quote, but he would not offer any information that would help Charlie get any kind of a "competitive fix" on them. After getting about as much information as he tactfully could, Charlie departed to prepare for meeting number two.

What negotiating tactics had Charlie employed in this first meeting? Well first of all he had begun with a high opening demand, and had not conceded anything this early despite the initial price resistance he had encountered. Secondly, he had established what Central's opening offer was, and had pushed for some sort of early concession on their part. He had also presented a credibility device in the form of a prepared contract for signature. And although Wattkins had sidestepped any concession, by pleading some concern over his vice-president's reaction, Charlie persisted by requesting to meet with that higher authority—thus, not letting Wattkins off the hook. Even after this was agreed to, Charlie had continued to gather additional information which would be useful in the next stage of the negotiation. So, all in all, Charlie had been doing a pretty decent job, from what we can observe, in applying some of the basic tools of effective sales negotiators. With information in hand Charlie went back to prepare for the next step by briefing his cost engineer, Jim Lanear, who would accompany Charlie in the forthcoming meeting with Mr. Wattkins and his vice-president.

The Major Bargaining Begins

It was agreed that Jim would take a very hard stance on engineering costs, and would in fact perform a "tough guy" role to soften-up the Central people as much as possible. Charlie would give him the signal when to back-off to let Charlie step in as "nice guy" to conduct the win-win part of the negotiation. This was accomplished early in that second meeting with Jim citing the proven accuracy of his cost analysis on two previous jobs they had performed for Central Utilities. He followed this by refusing to budge an inch on any estimate, and in fact he asked for a flexible cost-of-labor clause to be included in the proposal. He explained that there were "rumblings by one of the unions about guaranteed overtime, rumblings which might have to be placated." This tough approach seemed to take both Wattkins and the VP a bit off guard, for they had attempted to start the meeting off with a pretty hard stance of their own. But Jim played it well and kept the pressure on with a persistent, although not abrasive, adherence to both price and specs as originally proposed.

After the key points in the proposal had been talked through, without either side budging an inch, Jim again pushed for some sort of escalator clause on contract labor costs. The Central team stiffly rejected any such concession and when Jim felt he had pushed them far enough he suddenly shifted gears, backed off, and proceeded to pull out a stack of engineering data from his briefcase.

He presented a number of background statistics justifying the design time, the testing procedure and installation contingencies. But at no time did he get into detailed breakdowns of the various cost estimates. The VP tried testing him several times on cost details, but he was aware that Charlie and Jim were too professional as a negotiating team to reveal such confidential information. In exasperation he stated that as far as he was concerned they were at a standstill and "unless the sales proposal could be modified in some more acceptable fashion, they may as well call the whole thing off for the time being."

Up to this point Jim's "tough guy" role had put the customer on the defensive. Although he had not managed to pull any concessions out of the Central Utilities negotiating team he had warded off any meaningful attempts on their part to pressure himself and Charlie for price concessions. In accomplishing this, he had utilized the credibility device of citing precedents in his own record of preparing accurate proposals. He had even used an escalation tactic of pushing for a flexible labor cost, although it was purely a tactic, since neither he nor Charlie really expected any pressing demands from the union. Finally, Jim drew upon an array of statistics as a tactic to relieve some tension he had generated, and to move the discussion along into an area of data that he could control and perhaps use to influence this engineering-oriented VP.

Caucusing When Things Get Tough

Instead of retreating at this time Charlie suggested that the two sides caucus separately and that maybe after a phone call or two he and Jim would be better able to proceed in the discussion, if that were acceptable to the Central team. This was agreed to, and during the caucus Charlie and Jim concurred that Jim's "tough" role had served its purpose. Charlie would now move in to get things off dead center, and would try stroking the VP's ego with a compliment as to how highly he valued the long, businesslike working relationship they had enjoyed with Central Utilities. He would assure them that come what may, he clearly wanted "to work this out to the satisfaction of Central Utilities."

"One problem, however," he continued, "was that there had recently been some legal rumblings about his firm showing favoritism to two or three major utilities and that he might find it difficult to back off," from Jim's legitimate cost proposal, at least with his own management, at this time. Wattkins suggested that that was Charlie's problem, not Central's. Charlie countered that if his own legal department "got shaky" and put some constraints on him, it could affect the Central proposal—and that although he regretted it as much as Wattkins, he would certainly do everything in his power to arrive at a final proposal which would be acceptable to Central. Wattkins indicated his appreciation of Charlie's willingness to work it out, but asked specifically what

Charlie felt he could do to make the proposal more palatable considering Central's need to hold the cost down to a range of $260,000. At this point Charlie felt that he had the negotiation set up for a major breakthrough, with an offer to modify the proposal to Central's satisfaction in exchange for a major concession on the price.

Although not stated in the original request for quotation, Charlie knew that the earlier he could make delivery of the installation of equipment the greater the advantage to Central, because they had so many other things hinging on completion of this project. Therefore, he offered what seemed a major benefit to Central Utilities (was of practically no cost consequence at all to his people) of a four-week earlier completion date than the deadline originally discussed; this in exchange for a price commitment of $287,500. Wattkins and his VP had trouble hiding their enthusiasm at this concession, but the VP retained his aplomb sufficiently to make an immediate counter-offer of $270,000. Charlie paused for a moment on this one, then replied that he did not feel he could ever get that through his organization considering the hassle he would have to go through "to change production schedules and all."

Wattkins and the VP paused for a long time, scribbled some numbers down in front of each other, then countered with an offer of $272,000, provided Charlie and Jim would withdraw any flexible cost of labor clause from further consideration. Jim had been silent during this part of the bargaining since the caucus, but he gently offered at this point that that would be a difficult thing to agree to at a price of $272,000. Charlie agreed in an equally gentle tone of voice, and relieved any possible tension by scribbling some meaningless numbers in front of Jim to give the Central team a chance to think for a moment. Neither side appeared ready to offer any additional concessions at this time, and since it was almost noontime they agreed to break for lunch and reconvene at one-thirty, since they all had phone calls to make and other duties to attend to.

What had happened since the caucus had gone generally in Charlie's favor from the point at which he had conveyed a win-win desire by massaging the Central team's ego, followed by a sidestepping tactic involving reference to a stumbling block with his legal department which he attempted to introduce for credibility purposes. He had then managed his timing well by introducing a proposed change in the package with an earlier delivery, a minor concession to him, but a major benefit to his customer. In fact, he had not offered even that minor concession until he sensed it would buy him a significant concession in return, which it did in the form of $10,000. That was already

$5,000 above his minimum acceptable price objective. From that point on the concession curve moved very slowly, with Charlie holding at $6,370 below his original demand and Central Utilities at $12,000 above their original offer.

Shifting Gears at Lunch Break

During the long lunch-hour break Charlie quickly shifted into action. He made a key change in his negotiating team by releasing Jim, who had performed his "tough guy" role, and brought in Henry Pollock, the production manager, who would be in charge of the Central job, along with one of Henry's installation supervisors, the latter mostly for effect. Charlie's reasoning was that he could make a significant stride toward a win-win session in the afternoon if he moved out of the tough bargaining stance, involving his cost engineer, and into a problem-solving approach with his people who would actually be doing the work for Central Utilities.

Wattkins and his VP seemed to respond favorably as Charlie led the discussion into a series of "What if we change this" type probing questions, followed by a great deal of mutual exploring of detailed manufacturing and installation issues: "What if we reduce the weight by using this new type of insulator?" "Would you be willing to concede a little on the price if we agree to do some of the wiring at the plant, which you would normally have to do after installation?" "What if we agreed to do the most disruptive part of the installation on Saturday?"

Charlie had carefully avoided offering any "what-ifs" which might have resulted in any major expense. But he had clearly given the Central team some useful nuggets permitting them to make a couple of key price concessions with supporting rationale. In fact Charlie mentally calculated his incremental costs of these minor concessions at a total of $450, for which he gained another $6,000 in concessions from Wattkins raising their offer to $278,000. But Charlie was a very skilled negotiator and sensing that Central Utilities really preferred to do business with his organization, and knowing that they were under some time constraints to "get cracking," he was not about to take the comfortable way out. He was not settling for a net profit in the range of 9% when he had his sights set on something more in the range of 20%. Every thousand dollars he could add to that selling price now was an additional 1% net.

During the early afternoon session Charlie had made some more significant advances by changing his team makeup and by introducing his what-if probing tactics. He had converted a hard bargaining negotiation into a win-win problem-solving one. He had made some carefully calculated minor concessions, in return for which he had garnered some fairly major price concessions from this potential customer.

Team Consultation at Stretch

By mid-afternoon both teams were tired and readily agreed that it was time for a break. Although a great deal of progress had been made, neither was in a rush to give in to the other's demands just for the sake of wrapping up the agreement. Charlie welcomed the opportunity to chat in private with his team, since neither Henry nor the supervisor were experienced negotiators, and he wanted to make sure they were tuned into his strategy. It was important that no unnecessary information would be leaked during the inevitable weariness of the late afternoon. In fact, to guard against things slipping into a long, drawn-out, and unproductive lull in everybody's energy curve, Charlie decided to change the pace by introducing additional pressure via some "hurry-up" tactics. Since there were 17 key areas in the proposal, he explained to his team that he would begin pushing the VP pretty rapidly to initial each area, item by item, as soon as they reconvened. In this way they could "narrow down the areas for further negotiation to just two or three key items" including the final price, of course. Henry and his supervisor were to stay out of the bargaining unless called upon for specifics. Otherwise, Charlie would conduct all the discussion. This was agreed to so when the session resumed Charlie began pushing the Central VP to initial his agreement on 14 of the "pretty well agreed upon points." Charlie handled it well and the constant pressure, gently applied, eventually got all 14 items committed to, despite some definition clarification required on a couple of installation issues.

Things then began to get tough. After having clipped through the 14 "easy" commitments on various specs and routine clauses in an hour and a half, Central Utilities was not ready to agree to a price of $287,500, from which Charlie had not budged since very early-on in the bargaining. Nor were they in agreement with Charlie's demand for a 50% front-end payment, followed by three equal installments over the next three months. They also wanted a heavy penalty clause included in case of late installation. Although Charlie realized he would eventually have to agree to some kind of penalty clause, he had resisted with such tenacity he noticed at one point that Wattkins was getting quite annoyed. He had probably assured the VP he could get a stringent penalty built in for unforeseen delays. So Charlie eased off with the decision that he'd better take Wattkins off the hook, or risk messing up all the gains he had accomplished so far.

Charlie's pressure tactics had worked pretty well, but now he needed to shift gears again and give Wattkins some strokes. He expressed his "complete understanding for the need of having some penalty clause built in." His only concern was that since he had "already agreed to a four-week earlier delivery, a penalty clause would seem like a double blow" to his top management, and he was "getting concerned" about how quickly he could get the contract approved back in his own organization. This was "particularly true considering the need to move without delay." In any case, that was his "only concern." He was "very sympathetic" to Wattkins' request so "if the penalty date could be fixed at the original completion-of-installation date, four weeks after the new commitment date," he believed he could initial that right now.

This position seemed to mollify Wattkins and he even gave Charlie a genuine smile. His aggravation now over, he indicated he'd need to think about that for awhile. But that was as far as Charlie was able to get that afternoon. So, still a distance apart on the price and the payment schedule, the two teams decided to break off negotiations for the time being. Charlie's gamble was that they would no doubt be able to get back together within a couple of days.

Despite his desire to get this contract, Charlie's experience and negotiating skill had kept him from giving-in to the temptation of wrapping it up quickly in that grueling late-afternoon session. By this point many sales negotiators would have sacrificed much net profit due to their self-made vulnerability to pressure from a skilled opponent. Charlie had used some tactics to change the pace of the negotiating by speeding the bargaining along quickly through the easy issues. Then, having zeroed in on the toughies, he had very astutely stepped back and soothed his buyer's ego when he realized he had pushed too hard. And most interestingly, Charlie was willing to deadlock to avoid unnecessary concessions at the end of the day, a calculated risk which in his judgment would pay off.

Reconvening the Teams

At this point, Charlie's patience was rewarded. The next afternoon when he called Wattkins to touch base, a meeting was quickly arranged for the following morning between Wattkins, his vice-president, and Charlie, along with Charlie's production manager, Henry Pollock. For the first half hour of that meeting, Charlie and Henry said very little. They simply listened to Wattkins' summary of their agreements to date and his understanding of the positions of the two sides as they then stood. Charlie concurred with Wattkins' summary and asked if he could show some 35mm slides to help clarify lead time requirements.

He and Henry had used that previous "off day" to quickly convert a colorful PERT chart type presentation onto 30 sides which portrayed the critical design, manufacturing, and installation time segments required for the project. The professionalism of this tactic seemed to have at least some minor positive effect on the pair from Central Utilities. Charlie continued next by giving them each a supporting document summarizing the manufacturing procedure and safety policies to be adhered to during the three phases outlined in the slides.

After Henry had clarified a couple of technical questions, Charlie asked if they could now get agreement on the penalty clause issue. Following a short exchange, the two sides agreed to split the four-week cushion time Charlie had proposed in the previous session, and they agreed that the penalty, in case of a delayed installation, would take effect two weeks after the contract commitment date. This was only two weeks earlier than the original date of installation indicated in the initial sales proposal.

With the late delivery penalty clause agreed on, the only two items remaining were the payment schedule and the final price. The two sides both showed keen interest in whittling out a mutually acceptable payment schedule. They finally worked down to three equal payments over the same time span originally proposed by Charlie—an arrangement most satisfactory to him, and much easier for Central to cope with in terms of their present budget.

The final price, however, was not to be so quickly resolved. After a few minutes of discussion Wattkins offered a token additional $500 concession that left the respective demand and offer at $287,500 versus $278,500, a $9,000 gap. Charlie judged he could still gain some concessions. But Central stood firm for the next several minutes, clearly unwilling to offer further concessions unless Charlie could come up with some new rationale which might motivate them to budge. The only thing he could do at this point was to suggest a coffee break, advising them that he'd like to make a phone call back to his office.

During the one day recess, and this morning's session, Charlie had used patience as a key strategy. He had combined that with some effective listening. He had then pulled in a credibility device, exhibiting some professionally prepared slides and handout documents as supporting media. This had demonstrated some further credibility ammunition by detailing some necessary policies and procedures. Following this he did some give-and-take via tradeoffs on the payment schedule. He then held firm on the major bargaining issue by calling time-out for a break when it seemed the most appropriate thing to do to avoid jeopardizing the win-win momentum.

Conducting the Final Session

Although Charlie had had full bargaining authority throughout the entire negotiation, and his only reason for calling his office was a routine check for phone messages, he returned from the break with the dramatic news that he was now able to make a major concession by lowering the price to $284,750. The Central VP thanked Charlie for that "breakthrough," but expressed mild disappointment that the concession had not been somewhat larger. He then requested an additional $3,000. At this point Charlie knew he had them, for what the VP had unwittingly communicated, perhaps in his haste to get it wrapped up, was a counter-offer of $281,750. Charlie gently but clearly pointed this out. He then countered that he regretted that he had no further authority to concede.

In taking this position Charlie realized that he was taking a calculated risk, for he was forcing Central to accept as a final price the $284,750. To pull this off with a win-win feeling by both sides, he then took his negotiating opponents off the hook by offering them a face-saving $3,000 worth of "free" spare parts (which would cost him a total of about $1,000).

To Charlie's relief, and mild surprise, the two Central Utilities team members looked at each other, nodded, and smiled at Charlie, quickly and quietly confirming their final acceptance. Charlie promptly agreed and summarized the points of agreement in the contract.

After he and Wattkins had both initialed the contract copy, as amended, Charlie made one final attempt to add some value to the agreement by suggesting that it might be useful to Central Utilities to work out a routine preventive maintenance contract with him, "to cover, say the next three to five years of operation." Since routine maintenance was not considered a very critical item in this generally trouble-free type of equipment, neither side had mentioned it as a part of the contract. Wattkins responded that he felt Central's own maintenance program was probably adequate for that, but that if Charlie wanted to send him a draft of a maintenance contract he would study it and give it due consideration. Charlie indicated he would send such a draft the following day along with the final typed copy of the sales contract.

The negotiation was thus concluded, both sides expressing satisfaction with an acceptable contract and both looking forward to a mutually healthy working relationship between their two companies in the future. All 17 points in the contract had been thoroughly worked through between these two negotiating teams, to the mutual satisfaction of everybody. During this final stage of the bargaining Charlie had continued to demonstrate a high level of sales negotiating skills. He had used the tactic of pleading insufficient authority to grant the level of price concession the buyers requested, but having thus backed them into a corner he then eased them into a face-saving position by offering some "free" spare parts at a nominal cost to his own organization. After successfully engineering that critical phase, he had then quickly moved into a summary, and concluded the formal negotiating securing Central Utilities' commitment by simply initialing the draft contract they had been working on. Charlie had then attempted to gain additional value by peddling some extras in the form of a maintenance contract as a separate and additional revenue-producer. Charlie had indeed assessed his opponents' strengths and weaknesses and had pushed a very fine bargain for his organization.

He had employed a wide range of skills and tactics to accomplish his obviously high level of objectives. His opening demands, his use of limited authority, his ferreting out of critical information, his effective use of negotiating team members, for "tough guy" as well as credibility purposes, demonstrated the skill of an experienced sales negotiator. Charlie used time-related tactics throughout, and he managed to change the package at key points. He massaged his opponent's egos, used a sidestepping tactic or two, and even attempted to peddle some extra services at the end. Although Charlie had probably done a good job of planning and preparation, he clearly was also able to think and maneuver quickly as the situation had demanded.

Some Observations

In the description you have just read, the sales negotiator's willingness to take some reasonable risk was a very significant characteristic during his moment-to-moment decision-making in the face-to-face bargaining. Closely related to this was his patience, his willingness to walk out at critical times without a final commitment, his ability to resist that pressure to wrap it up. And closely related to his ability to use patience was his ability to listen, then to make use of what he had heard.

Fundamental to all that skillful use of bargaining tactics was the climate that was established and maintained, not automatically, but through the conscious effort of the sales negotiator. If Central Utilities in this case, had not sensed a cooperative win-win working relationship at the conclusion of the negotiation, rest assured Charlie's organization would, in the end, have paid a price for any dissatisfaction. It might have been in the form of delayed payments, or through claims filed, or through an unwillingness by the other party not to bend a little downline when something goes afoul. Or it may have been through any number of other ways a customer can use to get even. But whomever had come out ahead in the direct negotiation, it had been extremely good business to have given the other party a reason to sense a win-win.

Rate Yourself on Your Skill in Using Negotiating Tactics

How effective are you in using negotiating tactics in the face-to-face meeting with a buyer?

- Pressing for a large concession in spite of early resistance.
- Tactfully arranging to negotiate at the highest concession-making level possible.
- Avoiding making early concessions.
- Making it as easy as possible for the buyer to confirm agreement.
- Not rushing into an agreement before probing for information.
- Using your backup people in a targeted way.
- Employing a "tough guy" when appropriate.
- Calling time-out for a caucus when needed.
- Holding back on giving concessions until they are needed.
- Using tension-relievers at opportune times.
- Bringing in new support people at opportune times.
- Keeping on-track by summarizing and confirming easy-to-agree-to issues.
- Stroking the buyer's ego to relieve pressure.
- Using a variety of tactics.

- Having some face-savers ready when needed.
- Having some extras to peddle after the main negotiation is concluded.
- Taking some calculated risks.

9

HOW TO COUNTER
THE BUYER'S TACTICS

Seller:	"Thanks for bringing Burl into this. I have a much better understanding now of your critical timing needs in the service requests."
Purchasing Agent:	"Good. Now, how about those extra service call charges you've been hitting us with?"
Seller:	"I think Burl understands now that if they bring things to the attention of our service rep during our routine monthly call, it could save you at least one unnecessary service visit each month."
Purchasing Agent:	"Maybe, but you've been hitting us with at least three extra charges each month. I'd like to void these last six service invoices."
Seller:	"Well, you note that Burl admitted they've been putting new people on that job recently with no training at all. Things are bound to jam up when new people don't understand the handling steps Burl mentioned."
Purchasing Agent:	"Why don't you credit us on these six, and we'll start with a clean slate?"
Seller:	"Tell you what. Next time our service rep is scheduled here, we'll give your new people a one-hour training session on handling steps. That will boost your efficiency, in addition to reducing unnecessary service calls. I can work out the details with Burl."

Purchasing Agent:	"That's fine—and let's just cancel these past three service invoices then, instead of all six."
Seller:	"Burl said he'd be happy to pay them—if we can just solve his problem. And we can do that. Look, we'll credit this last one, and schedule the training at Burl's earliest convenience. Okay?"
Purchasing Agent:	"Okay. I guess we can live with that for this time."

PUT YOURSELF IN THE BUYER'S SHOES

It is easy to think of everybody in the buyer organization as representing a single opinion, all in agreement. That isn't necessarily so. The purchasing agent is apt to be quite different from the people who will actually use your product. They will differ in skills, in priorities, and in attitudes. The purchasing people are more likely to be highly skilled negotiators and more concerned with the best possible price. The product users may or may not be skilled negotiators, may give more priority to quality and service, and may be in conflict with their own purchasing people. It is important for you as the seller to sense these differences, have a feel for whose opinion will carry the most weight, and deal with each person based on his role and his priorities. The fact that a purchasing agent is adamant that you not go around him does not remove the opportunity to address that product user's priorities. Indeed, giving the purchasing agent the ammunition he needs to negotiate internally with his own product users is a critical part of the negotiating process.

The purchasing agent typically negotiates almost daily. One of the key measurements on which the purchasing agent is evaluated is on dollars saved. And on this count, it is important that he looks good to his own management. It follows, then, that you may not be doing the purchasing agent a favor by starting out with a discounted price. On the contrary, he needs to go back to his own people and say, "Here was the initial price, but here is a lower price I was able to negotiate."

The product user, on the other hand, may not even be aware of the negotiating process. Some are. Don't generalize. But if you need to rely on the purchasing agent as your link with the user, then prepare to give the purchasing agent some concessions in areas like quality and service to make it easier for him to negotiate with his own users.

Technical people in the buyer organizations will frequently specify much higher performance requirements than they will ever need.

Purchasing professionals are aware of this. Because of this, there is internal conflict and negotiating going on in that buyer organization before and during your own negotiations with them. When an inexperienced sales negotiator becomes aware of this, he is sometimes tempted to go around the purchasing agent and deal directly with the user. Now, working directly with the user is a good strategy, but that can be dangerous to attempt after a conflict has begun between the user and his own purchasing people. The time to initiate user contact is before that internal conflict. If the purchasing agent perceives that you and his own user are ganging up on him, you'd best hope you never have to deal with that purchasing agent again.

This all suggests that it is very useful to try to find out what the user's spending authority is, and under what circumstances does company policy require him to go through his own purchasing department. Once you understand that buyer organization's internal practices, you are in a position to apply the right strategies and right tactics to the right people at the right time.

Let's Listen In

Jackie is the new quality control manager at a large office products manufacturing company. Last week she asked, Robin, her boss, for permission to buy three new measuring instruments, one for each of three recently expanded production lines. Robin agreed and asked her to process a routine purchase order so that the purchasing department could "get cracking on it quickly."

"Robin, if I go through purchasing, they will go out and buy the cheapest instruments from the lowest bidder. We just can't afford that risk."

"Jackie, that's why it's critical that you provide very clear specifications with your request to purchasing. I know they'll probably come back and question you on the specs, but that's their job. In the end you write the specs, not them."

"Robin, we just can't write specifications on these kinds of instruments for some of the most critical things—things like service quality and recalibration frequency. Those things are absolutely critical! Sure, any vendor can promise to perform good service, even in writing. But you know what it's like to deal with a second-rate vendor on something like this. Purchasing doesn't understand this, and frankly, my experience with them is they don't really want to understand. All they are concerned with is the lowest price."

"Well, Jackie, that isn't necessarily true. I understand your point, but purchasing can be quite helpful. Besides, the boss wants us to go through channels and to use purchasing according to policy."

"I'm not trying to violate policy. In fact, if I buy each instrument as a separate purchase, I'm well within our spending authority limits. Robin, you know very well if this goes to purchasing, they'll wind up buying instruments from somebody like Southern Apparatus. The instruments will be out of calibration every other month, and it will be like pulling teeth to get them out here for servicing. How do you write that into a purchase order and have any faith in it?"

And So On...

Let's interrupt here and assume that in the end Robin insisted that Jackie go through channels.

As the sales negotiator for a higher quality instrument company, how would you best handle this one? If you could have established contact with Jackie before she was ever forced to go through purchasing, you might have helped her write specifications into the order—specifications which only your instruments could meet. But if you try that strategy after she has processed the purchase order, you may get yourself into all kinds of hot water with a skeptical purchasing agent.

This is not a condemnation of purchasing agents as having a single-minded, "price is the only issue" mentality. Most purchasing departments are quite quality sensitive. This is simply to illustrate one kind of conflict that operates within the organizations you are trying to sell. How you negotiate with that organization depends on who you are talking to and what their own priorities are. There is no cookbook recipe as to how you find out these things about your buyers. Our goal here is to arouse your awareness that these internal conflicts are happening constantly, and it will strengthen your negotiating position if you take time to find out about them through every means at your disposal.

Analyzing the Buyer Organization

To analyze who to deal with in the buyer organization, ask yourself these questions:

1. Who are all the key players in the buyer organization with vested interests in this negotiation?
2. Who in my organization would be the best person to contact, and to probe, each of those players?

3. What are their probable concerns and priorities?

4. What strategies should I use to influence each key player as early as possible?

Rate Yourself on Your Understanding of the Buyer Organization

How effective are you at "getting inside" the buyer organization?

- Learning exactly who will be using, re-working, or reselling your product or service.

- Addressing both the purchasing person's needs and that user's needs.

- Understanding the decision-making process, policies, and procedures in their organization.

- Dealing with internal differences and conflicts in their organization.

- Finding diplomatic ways to influence others in their organization without offending your primary contact.

Buyer: "You'll have to reduce the price by at least $6,000. The software is inadequate."

Seller: "I understand, Wiggins. Our price is fairly firm. But we can surely do some software adaptations for you."

Buyer: "Look. Here are 200 pages of technical specs. It'll be easier for us both if you just reduce the price by $6,000, and let us deal with the software."

Seller: "We've handled a wide variety of software specifications. Let me bounce these off our design people. I'm confident they'll give you what you need."

Buyer: "I don't have the authority to give you a set of these specs."

Seller: "Could your manager do that?"

Buyer: "Yes. But look, we either have to reach an agreement on price right now, or I'll have to go back for another committee approval."

Seller: "Let's do this. Let's sign the agreement based on the price and conditions in the proposal. We'll add a clause committing us to adapt the software to your specifications."

Buyer: "You vendors are all alike. I doubt you have the know-how to do that."

Seller: (smiling) "We've done it for the three most demanding organizations in the field. Give us a try."

COUNTER-TACTICS IN SALES NEGOTIATIONS

In the last chapter we looked at an illustration of some sales negotiating tactics in action. Let's switch sides now and put the emphasis on counter-tactics as employed by successful sales negotiators. We separate tactics from counter-tactics here only for purposes of illustrative emphasis. Naturally, in actual negotiations, they are intertwined with the negotiator's shifting of gears from moment-to-moment to maneuver or to react to the situation at hand.

If tactics and counter-tactics are applied intelligently, there can usually be a better bargain for both sides. But in the process of searching for that mutually better solution, the sales negotiator must be adept at countering the various tactics and ploys the prospective buyers may employ.

For every tactic there is one or more counter-tactics to consider. At the end of Chapter 6 some of the issues in preparing to use counter-tactics were explored. But, as with tactics, preparing to negotiate effectively and actually doing it in the heat of battle involve two separate and distinct sets of skills.

Taking Another Look at Climate

The more positive or constructive the negotiating climate, the less onerous the task of employing counter-tactics. Since by definition, a counter-tactic is in response to a tactic, the more aggressive the buyer's tactics the greater the burden on the salesperson to respond quickly with effective counter-tactics. Aggressive tactics may of course be subtle, and almost covert, but prompt reaction is nevertheless important if the climate is highly competitive or win-lose in nature. Thus, if a win-win climate is desired by the sales team, the better the preparation and fostering of cooperative attitudes on both sides in advance of the bargaining, the easier the burden of counter-tactics.

Not all tactics need to be countered. If the other side employs a tactic which is not in conflict with your own negotiating objectives it may be best to tactfully ignore it and let it rest. Indeed many buyer's tactics complement some of your selling objectives, in which case you would build on them rather than attempt to counter them. This is all to point out the importance of having a very clear understanding of your specific negotiating objectives and strategies. Know exactly where you stand at any given point in the bargaining before you react to a tactic with an appropriate counter-tactic—if it is appropriate to react at all. If in your preparation you have anticipated the tactics the prospect or buyer is apt to employ, and the likely counter-tactics you will use, it is critical that you not let yourself and your team get into a rigid mind-set. That may inhibit you from revising your earlier perceptions as the situation demands. The face-to-face negotiating may often involve many surprises in both tactics and opposing strategies, good surprises and bad, again calling for prompt and flexible response by you or your team. In a negotiation involving a series of face-to-face meetings it is desirable to revise between sessions, and to replot any earlier plans outlining anticipated tactics and counter-tactics to be used.

In thinking through and in applying counter-tactics the critical thing is to avoid using a heavy-handed counter-tactic which may gain a momentary point but cost you dearly in your overall strategy to steer the opposing negotiators into a win-win course. If win-win is your strategy the best counter-tactic is one which positions the discussion into a mutual problem-solving direction. If the other side is persistent with aggressive tactics that tend to force you into a losing position, it may take considerable time, discipline, and effective counter-tactics to move them into a more rational mode. In this case it becomes a matter of judgment as to the value of your time versus the potential benefits of a mutually satisfactory conclusion.

Defending with Counter-Tactics in Different Market Positions

One of the things that affects the kinds of tactics a sales negotiator may need to counter is the kind of market you're in. Is it a buyers' market, a sellers' market, or a balanced market? Knowing this will help you to determine the kinds of strategies, tactics, and resulting counter-tactics to anticipate.

1. *In a buyers' market.* This is the toughest situation to cope with because the buyer can always go to another seller if he doesn't like your offer. However, if it is just a temporary buyers' market, and a longer-term working relationship with you may be advantageous to him, don't automatically give in to his demands and strong-arm tactics. Even if he is the sole outlet or prospect for whatever you are selling, and even if his tactics seem to leave you with little to negotiate, it is the true test of an effective sales negotiator to move with confidence, probing for every opportunity to lower his perceived targets while maintaining your own.

The most difficult tactics to deal with in a buyers' market are time-related tactics, because time is on his side. If you don't make sufficient concessions quickly enough, the prospective buyer may decide to shop around. The buyer may attempt to force a quick concession curve, or use deadlocks, time-outs, speed-ups, and slow-downs. He may employ interminable patience in putting time pressure on the salesperson. If the market is extremely in the buyer's favor he can easily open with very high demands and vigorously resist making any concessions, even raising his demands during the course of the bargaining by requesting various changes in the package to his benefit.

This may sound all too obvious and hopeless, but not necessarily so. Remember, for every tactic there is at least one appropriate counter-tactic. It is a poor sales negotiator who does not attempt at least one counter-tactic to test the validity and the resolve of the buyer's demands. After all, even in a buyers' market, most buyers are not unscrupulous scoundrels. Many will accept the sincere attempts of the seller to strike a win-win bargain.

2. *In a balanced market.* Since few markets are totally to the advantage of either the buyer or the seller, some sort of balanced market is

probably most typical. It is certainly where the most opportunity exists for the negotiating skills of both sides to be tested. And it offers the greatest range of possible negotiating tactics and counter-tactics to be employed.

High-level opening demands, time pressure tactics, information probing, requests for changes in the package, appeals to higher authority, various decoys and team role tactics, nice-guy/tough-guy ploys, and the digging for miscellaneous extras at the end are all potential buyer tactics you must contend with and counter effectively.

3. *In a sellers' market.* This situation is the easiest to deal with from the point-of-view of counter-tactics by the seller. If the prospect with which you are now negotiating doesn't make satisfactory concessions, you can always sell it to somebody else. But again, even if you are a sole source supplier, weigh your counter-tactics carefully for their longer range impact on your future negotiations.

How to Use Counter-Tactics for Every Occasion

The counter-tactics you choose to employ should be in concert with your specific negotiating objectives, strategies, and climate expectations. At least, they should not conflict with those basic aspects of the negotiation. It is again important to have a good handle on where you stand with those three fundamentals at all times during the bargaining. It's not always all that clear as things unfold, but it is important not to detract from a primary strategy by reacting inappropriately to a single irrelevant, or misplaced, tactic which a buyer has inadvertently slipped in. For example, if things are progressing reasonably well along a win-win course, and out of the blue one of the junior members of the buyer's negotiating team blurts out an aggressive and demeaning attack on one aspect of your sales proposal, it is not necessarily a signal for you to respond with a tough counter-tactic.

So keeping overall strategy and climate concerns in mind, let us look for a moment at some situations involving typical buyer tactics, addressing a few of the counter-tactic possibilities for consideration:

1. *Time pressure.* It's late Friday afternoon. You've been in heavy negotiations for two days to sell a million pounds of product to this major buyer. You must reach a commitment within the next half hour or lose the opportunity. Although you have only gone from a price of 98 cents a pound to 96 cents, he is now threatening to conclude the negotiation if you don't reduce it to 93 cents per pound. This would be

a penny below your minimum acceptable level. If you decide he's bluffing, your counter-tactic can be simply a patient rephrasing of your request for his commitment, taking care to avoid any blunt demands that may anger him. But if you decide that he is indeed willing to deadlock, you may need to try a combination of counter-tactics. Firstly, if there is any way to change the package as far as terms of payment, delivery schedules, future commitments, temporary warehousing, handling, containers, or any other aspect, however minor, as long as it does not involve major expense to you, now is the time to offer it.

Also, in countering this buyer's tactic of threatening deadlock to force you into a major concession as the deadline draws near, it is often very effective to make a rational plea to the effect of describing the damage you will realize by bowing to his demands. A gentle reminder of the possible negative implications on longer range relationships, followed by a play on his ego may help. (Recognize his "reputation for reasonableness.") Two things to avoid at a time like this is (a) making a significant concession before the briefcases have been closed, and before the "final" handshake has occurred. You can always turn around on your way out the door and agree to a concession after all—and (b) failing to hold some nuggets back for last-minute concessions if they should be required as counter-tactics against heavy time pressure tactics. Although effective employment of counter-tactics against time pressure may require quick spur-of-the-moment thinking, a bit of preparation and strategy planning will give you those nuggets for use at such critical times.

Another application of time-related tactics a buyer may employ involves the use of early deadlocks, delays and time-outs, all for the purpose of forcing a seller into tight time constraints later on when a deadline will be approaching. These antics, too, can be systematically countered by forcing an even earlier "psuedo-deadline" than the buyer expected, in effect gaining some cushion time for yourself. Appealing to higher authority, perhaps through our own higher management chain, can neutralize time pressure tactics. Withdrawing the offer, if you can risk it, or by offering a time-limited concession (i.e. must be accepted by a specified date or will be withdrawn), or by a combination of any of these are useful counter-tactics to the buyer's time-related tactics.

On the other hand, your prospective buyer may try some hurry-up tactics on you to get an attractive set of concessions quickly, purportedly giving you a deadline. It may be a genuine deadline, or it may simply be a tactic to rush you into a major concession. Patience, careful probing, and systematic information-gathering are appropriate counter-tactics to use.

2. *High opening demands.* Whether the buyer is using high-pressure, time-related tactics, or exceptionally high opening demands in the form of an unacceptably low price offer, stringent specs, or other very tough demands, one option the sales negotiator always has, of course, is to get emotional. Express some frustration in order to pique the buyer's sense of fair play. Emotionalism has certainly worked many times as an effective counter-tactic in negotiations but it must be used very sparingly. It must come across as absolutely genuine, and will only be effective on buyers who indeed have a sense of fair play, and who are in a position to practice it.

Perhaps a more commonly applicable set of counter-tactics to those exceptionally high targets the buyer has announced, involves a combination of patient, systematic problem-solving efforts. The first counter-tactic of course, is to stand by your own opening demands, but with an attitude of "let's explore this thing together." Remember, however hard-nose that opposing buyer team appears to be, if they can be persuaded of the value to them in seeking a mutually acceptable price and/or conditions of sale, they will ordinarily begin to participate with you in a joint problem-solving approach. To persuade a very difficult buyer of that value may require a fairly steady flow of counter-tactics from a straightforward rational plea right through an outright deadlock and walkout.

In countering a buyer who begins with an extremely low price offer, or very stringent conditions, and who sticks to his original set of demands like a bulldog, it is useful to have thought through which counter-tactics you will apply in order of increasing pressure. For example, you begin by gently refraining from any concessions from your own high demands. Follow this with a series of fact-finding probes to relate any benefits you are hitting them with to the requirements they are revealing. Then respond to any objections or resistance they raise with more benefit-related explanations and any minor concessions or inexpensive changes in the package to draw out larger counter-concessions from them. *But,* if they are not responding, you then need to counter more heavily with any information-gathering tactics possible. Use tactics such as phone calls, even purported phone calls back to the office; "tough guys" brought into your team to help hold the line in any vulnerable areas of your package; demands for counter-concessions on their part; appeals to higher authority; and most effectively, time pressure tactics, if they are under any kind of time pressure at all. And although direct attacks on competitor alternatives the buyer may be considering are traditionally taboo, it is important to seek ways to convey any genuinely adverse information about competitor service or products. Do this in an indirect or behind-the-scenes fashion if necessary; but to let a potential buyer unwittingly buy an inferior contract or package from a competitor due to insufficient information is not in his best interest, or yours, and would be an unforgivable neglect of counter-tactics on the part of a professional sales negotiator.

3. *Information barrages and voids.* If the buyer team attempts to bombard you with masses of technical, financial, or other data to rationalize their demands, you have basically three counter-tactics to employ: (a) deny its relevance and application to this negotiation, (b) patiently refer it all to your own experts for analysis, or (c) ignore it by diverting the thrust of the discussions to other issues. If, on the other hand, your prospective buyers are tight-lipped and refuse to share with you vital information, you may need to counter with the same array of patience and pressure counter-tactics outlined in dealing with "high opening demands."

4. *Changes in the package.* (Tactic) "Charlie, we like your product, and I think we have the price down to a level that I can at least go back to my management and talk about. But we must have a faster delivery schedule than you guys seem willing to offer." (Counter-tactic) "We definitely want to work that out, Jeff. I see you will be reshipping some of these units to your Alpha plant, which is within a hundred miles of our warehouse. If we could deliver the first two shipments to Alpha we could improve the schedule by one week on each delivery. We could then ship the remaining five back here to your main facility easily within your schedule requirements."

(Tactic) "We simply can't live with these terms of payment Charlie. Seven days net is ridiculous." (Counter-tactic) "Ms. Collins, if we could ship this by truck, and not have to bear air freight charges, I might be able to get those terms extended. You'd still have the stuff in plenty of time."

(Tactic) "I'm afraid we've hit an impasse Charlie. We'd like to have your buildings. We like your design features, and we know your quality, but $420,000 per building just won't fly." (Counter-tactic) "Pat, all through these discussions I've wondered about a couple of these design features. That is, do you people really need a second lavatory installed at the south end of each building, or could we eliminate those, since your personnel will rarely be working at that end of the buildings. Secondly, I really wonder if we couldn't eliminate the over-head conveyor track from those last two bays. All-in-all we could prob-ably reduce that $20,000 by at least another $6,000 to $7,000" ($8,000 to $9,000 in fact, but you don't offer the total concession in one chunk).

(Tactic) "Charlie, we wouldn't even consider paying this price. Your specs are far below our normal procurements. Cut about 20% off and maybe we can do business." (Counter-tactic) "Mr. Kline, maybe we can do something with the specs. If you could fill me in a bit on the applications you make with our equipment—the materials grades you're working with, the tolerances, and the like." (Probe!)

In the first situation above, Charlie got hit with what could have been a "diversionary" tactic. But it may also have been legit. Whatever it was, he came back with an innovative idea to change the package in a way which would not cost his organization any concessions, and which could provide a perfectly acceptable service to his customer. In the second situation, he countered a "tough guy" tactic with an offer to make a tradeoff, which should not only get Ms. Collins shipments to her in time, while offering her some relief on the terms of payment, but save his own organization a lot of money on shipping costs. A critical learning point to make right here is to note that Charlie has not blurted out all these great innovative ideas as soon as he thought of them. He held them back until he needed them as counter-tactics to avoid having to make expensive concessions at the demands of a skilled buyer-negotiator. Note that in the negotiation with Pat, Charlie might well have seen early on in the discussions that Pat's organization did not really need the extra lavatories and overhead track. But he did not offer these changes in the package too early. This enabled him to offer a contract price reduction when those changes were needed as counter-tactics to the threatened "deadlock" on price. This was a tactic Pat may have employed in order to get a major concession toward the end of the negotiation. But Charlie countered it effectively. In the final situation, Charlie effectively countered Mr. Kline's demand for a price concession by probing for more detailed information about Kline's "real" spec requirements, i.e., he did not fall into the assump-tion trap that the stated specs were the real or mandatory specs based on the buyer's actual requirements.

5. *Authority levels issues.* One problem faced by many salespeople every now and then is that of walking into an account to negotiate a price increase on a product or a service the account has been buying for some time. The purchasing rep or buyer will oftentimes put up

some pretty stiff resistance, even resorting to tactics like outrage and storms of indignation. This may require little more than "patience" as an effective counter-tactic. But frequently the tactic of "I don't have the 'authority' to pay such an inflated price" will be employed. The first response to this should be to probe for any information which might shed some light as to the real limit of his authority and as to any clues regarding recent competitor pricing activity. If he persists in the lack of authority tactic, you may need to (counter-) tactfully suggest that your higher management meet with the buyer's higher management to get the negotiating at a level where some (concession) decisions can be made. One of two things will probably happen: (a) the buyer will agree to this as a useful step, or (b) he will back off his lack of "authority" tactic if it was nothing more than a tactic, and will no doubt move into other tactics. Hopefully this will open the door to more "information probing" counter-tactics leading you into a problem-solving approach.

"Patience," and requesting to meet with "higher authority" levels, are only two appropriate counter-tactics for use against the "lack of authority" tactic. Practically all tactical negotiating issues are situational; i.e., the appropriate counter-tactics may be selected from the whole range of time pressures, tough guys, asking for counter-concessions, diversionary maneuvers, changing the package, etc., depending on the particulars of the situation.

6. *Ego attacks and massages.* If the opposing team is working on the ego of one of your team members, either by systematically attempting to tear down his confidence, or conversely, by deviously pumping him up for the soft kill, it is usually not appropriate to respond with counter-ego tactics. The purpose of ego-type tactics by a skilled opponent is to gain a concession by way of a nonrational influence on one of your decision-makers. The appropriate counter-tactic then, is one which will move the bargaining back into a rational decision-making or problem-solving mode. This no doubt requires that universal counter-tactic, "patience." But it also calls for a systematic probing and focus on specific and relevant information.

A skilled negotiator will work on your ego, positively or negatively. The key thing to keep in mind, once you are aware of this, is to discipline yourself and your team to resist the emotional influences by sticking to an "information focus." This kind of situation is blatantly obvious in many labor contract negotiations where ego attacks are common. In business negotiations they may be blatant. Certain buyers consciously play the nasty role for that very purpose. But it's the more subtle ego pressures, both sweet strokes and attacks, that require a constant attention to self-discipline to avoid giving away those precious concessions. A sugar-sweet negotiating opponent is after the same thing a nasty one is, and that is maximum concessions from the other side.

7. *Diversions, traps, and other irrelevancies.* "Charlie, this material you sold us didn't even begin to meet our performance specs. We had to destroy an entire batch. I expect your people to reimburse me for the full value, plus all my related operating costs and lost profits!" Of course this buyer hadn't told you that he was going to use your materials in an application for which they were never designed. Countertactics: set yourself a high objective (like "zero" reimbursement); concede very slowly and diplomatically; and probe for enough information to permit him to openly convince himself, in a face-saving way, that any adjustment you make is a real favor to him, since he had misused your product in his application. A buyer who has gotten himself trapped into an uncomfortable position may try all sorts of forceful or diversionary tactics to get a seller to negotiate with him. While you may need to help him, and to let him save face, you need not let him spoof you into making expensive concessions.

8. *Team manipulations.* Let's say you are negotiating with a prospective distributor to sell him the exclusive franchise to handle all of your business, sales, plus a lucrative service market, for a remote territory which you find demands entirely too much time and attention by both your sales and your service staff. First thing you know, your prospective franchisee who initially seemed to be most anxious to obtain the franchise, brings in a "tough guy" lawyer. He hammers away at you, not on big impact issues, but on a dozen little clauses, each of which could cost you a percentage point in net profits later on. He then sticks his accountant on you who proceeds to put you to work for the next three months digging out supporting data you had never maintained in the format he requests. Your prospect follows that with a bunch of requests for sales service support efforts "just to begin getting my people oriented." Just as his whole organization is about to drive you into a hasty decision in their favor (just to get the whole thing off your back), you realize you should have been countering their every tactic all along the way. But you were blinded by your pressing desire to get this top-notch distributor contracted as your exclusive franchise operator. In retrospect you now see that his lawyer and his accountant and his sales service people had functioned as a very effective negotiating team, wearing you down step-by-step. Every time they had hit you with

a tactic which you had failed to counter effectively, they were spurred on to hit you with another, until they now have you at a point where if you let the negotiations collapse, you lose.

9. *Tough guys need to be tested.* You've got to realize that this business of negotiating is an art and a process in which you need to participate in order to come out ahead—especially in a win-win—and that a "tough guy" strategy, and its related tactics, is only a part of the game. So don't get your hackles up and go cutting off your nose to spite your face. Negotiate, for goodness sake! Use some patience, some facts, some ego-boosters, and a few other counter-tactics, until you discover the right combination to bring this "toughie" or his team leader around to your advantage—and his as well, if that's possible.

10. *Counter for some extras.* If asking for a bunch of extras to add some net value, after the major issues have been resolved, is an appropriate tactic for the buyer to use, then it is of equally appropriate value for the seller to use, in reverse. Every time that buyer asks for some free service or parts or supplies thrown in at the end, you counter with a "standard price" for that extra, or a request to leave something else out of the package. Use tradeoffs like costly shipping modes, special packing, installation service, and the like.

11. *Validity testing.* When a skilled buyer uses a tactic for the purpose of maneuvering a seller into making a concession it is a cardinal rule of effective sales negotiating that the seller test the validity of that tactic with some counter-tactics. Whatever the tactic, the combination of appropriate counter-tactics will usually include some "information gathering" via probing questions. In negotiations we rarely have all the information we need. Thus every time the prospective buyer appears to have backed you against the wall, it is useful to counter with a rational information-gathering question. "Can you tell us a little more about the time cycle of your application of our products, Mr. Ward?" Information-gathering is a beautiful counter-tactic to employ whenever you sense the need to test the validity of what the buyer is trying to make you believe, or whenever it seems that your back is against the wall. "Well now what is the frequency of that demand situation Ms. Garrison, and is it at all predictable so we could maybe allow for it in our inventory planning?" Perhaps the most important thing to say about counter-tactics is simply "remember to use them."

COUNTER-TACTICS IN SUMMARY

There is a great deal written and said about the importance of assertiveness in both personal and commercial relationships. Assertiveness does not mean abrasiveness. In a very similar way that's what tactics and counter-tactics are all about. The sales negotiator must be sufficiently assertive to employ some appropriate counter-tactics to test a buyer's resolve. This is not limited to highly aggressive negotiations, which do occur despite our interest in fostering longer range win-win working relationships.

Counter-tactics are used to get to the heart of the issue, or to divert attention away from weaknesses, or to defuse risky confrontations, and for many other purposes. However they are used they should be in concert with those one or two key objectives, and related strategies, that must be successfully negotiated to arrive at a winning result. Counter-tactics can be planned to a degree, but for the most part they must be generated by an effective negotiator in many a situation which has not been anticipated and which calls for adept response to make maximum opportunity of the ever-changing events in the course of a negotiation.

Counter-Tactics

To respond effectively to typical tactics listed in the left-hand column, try some of the counter-tactics listed to the right.

Tactics	Counter-Tactics
Deadlocks: Time Pressure	Change the "Package" Patient Rephrasing Minor Concession Pseudo Deadline Appeal Higher Up Probe
Very Low Offers: Stringent Demands	Systematic Problem Solving Emotionalism Stand Firm Temporary Deadlock Probe Minor Concessions Delay "Tough" Guys
Barrages of Technical & Financial Data	Deny Relevance Refer to Experts Ignore & Refocus Discussion
Changes in the "Package"	Creative Alternatives Offer Tradeoffs Probe
Lack of Authority	Patient Probes Appeal Higher Up Change the "Package"
Ego Attacks & Massages	Patient Probes
Diversions	Probe Save Face Stand Firm
Team Manipulations	Probe Stand Firm
Tough Guys	Patience Credibility Information Ego-Boosters
Asking for Extras	Standard Charges Tradeoffs
Other Concession Pressures	Probe for Validity

Rate Yourself on Use of Counter-Tactics

How effective are you at resisting negotiating tactics with appropriate counter-tactics?

- Applying counter-tactics which match the negotiating climate.
- Ignoring or sidestepping tactics which may be contrary to the desired climate.
- Avoiding destructive counter-tactics which may only gain short-term advantage.
- Using some counter-tactics, even in a very weak position.
- Holding back some "nuggets" to be used as counter-tactics when needed.
- Combining patience with most counter-tactics.
- Generating creative alternatives and solutions as counter-tactics.
- Countering difficult tactics by probing for more information.
- Refocusing buyer's attacks into a problem-solving mode.
- Testing the validity of buyer tactics based on assumptions only.
- Maintaining control and momentum with positive counter-tactics.

10

GAINING
COMMITMENT

Seller: "Okay, Lanny, we agree on the price, the payment schedule, and the deliveries. The only thing left is this warranty period."

Buyer: "We've got to have one year. Six months is unacceptable."

Seller: "If you were using this indoors, we'd certainly go along with that. But I just can't sell one year to my management for a year-round outdoor installation."

Buyer: "You only come out here twice a year. I was hoping we could wrap this up this visit. My director simply won't go for a six-month warranty."

Seller: "Lanny, you've said our price is competitive. The three-phase payment schedule is acceptable to us. In turn, you've agreed to spreading the deliveries over six weeks. Neither of us want to let this warranty issue block the rest of the agreement."

Buyer: "I agree. How about if we write it for nine months then?"

Seller: "Lanny, you have negotiated the best agreement I've offered in many a month. I'm willing to offer that because we trust you. But the warranty is something I just can't bend on under these conditions."

Buyer: "Would you really go back home empty-handed?"

Seller: "I sure don't want to, Lanny. But I just can't give on this one."

Buyer: "Okay. I'll live with it."

Seller: "Great. Thanks, Lanny. Let's shake on it."

Buyer: "Oh, incidentally. Could you throw in a set of those calibration tools?"

Seller: "We can pack them with the first shipment. Here's a copy of
the price list for those, along with a set of instructions."

GAINING COMMITMENT

There are a lot of sales representatives who do a perfectly acceptable job of preparation, and who make a nice, smooth sales
presentation, but who somehow can't seem to "close" a very high percentage of calls. The same thing seems to apply to negotiations, but
unfortunately in a more subtle, and oftentimes more costly way. It is
very easy to gain commitment if, as the seller, you are prepared to use
your authority to agree to most of the concessions demanded by the
prospective buyers.

However, the purpose of a sales negotiator is to gain "a highly
desirable" commitment, hopefully for both sides, and not just to gain
"a" commitment. The difficulty is that so often the people with the
authority are not the people with the negotiating skills. Hence, they
indeed gain a commitment, much to the satisfaction of the buyer organization. In a sense they are as faulty as the sales rep who fails to close.
Oh, they close all right—much like the basketball player, who in the
heat of the contest, inadvertently tips the ball into the opposing basket.
The issue at hand is that it takes more than authority to gain an
"effective" commitment.

There are two sides to that negotiated commitment: The substantive side—i.e., the measureable values in terms of price, time, etc.; and
the psychological side—i.e., the egos and the feelings of satisfaction
gained by each party to the agreement. It is important to keep both
sides in balance as the negotiation nears closure if genuine commitment is to occur. It is also important for bridging into future negotiations, not only for repeat business from that same buyer, but for word-
of-mouth advertising to other prospective buyer organizations as well.
Or, another way of expressing it might be "to drive a hard bargain
takes skill, but to drive a hard bargain and make the other party feel
good about it takes class." Ideally we need to strive for both outcomes
in our negotiated sales agreements.

12 Key Points in Gaining Commitment

There are a number of areas to consider as we get down to the
wire in a negotiation. Once the tug-of-war and the conflict and the
jockeying for position stage is over, and basic agreement seems to be a

possibility, several factors begin to come to a head. Are we bending too far? Have we pushed hard enough? Are our key team members all on the same wavelength? Will our credit and collections people buy this, and will their marketing people go along with that? In assessing the many gray areas that can and do arise as the moment of final commitment approaches, a systematic check of the following key areas is useful.

1. *Do you really want to reach this agreement?* Ordinarily we don't enter into the time-consuming process of a negotiation unless we have some expectation of reaching an agreement, a contract, or a sale. During the course of the negotiation, however, new information or new situations can arise which may prompt us to re-examine our original objectives. From what we have learned about the prospective buyer organization, have we found that our long-range payoff may be marginal? Has some new opportunity to deal with another organization on a more favorable basis suddenly been presented? Has our capability to deliver been adversely affected by some recent events? Are some of the buyer organization's demands of dubious legal or ethical concern? Have we been unwittingly bargained into an unacceptable level of projected net profit or cash flow bind? A final reassessment of the desirability of reaching a binding agreement is often appropriate, if any doubtful areas exist, before getting down to the final handshakes and signatures in any sales negotiation.

2. *What are the key issues?* In Chapter 8 we observed that Charlie went through a process of zeroing in on three critical issues by taking some time to summarize the other 14 items on which he and Central Utilities seemed to have agreement. This approach not only focuses the bargaining on the key areas for discussion, but it also emphasizes the great area of agreement already achieved. This casts a positive, or optimistic, tone to the overall negotiation, thereby fostering a win-win climate as the difficult bargaining moves into its final stages. In fact, if the areas of agreement and mutual benefit tend to be on major issues, such as price or technology, it is wise to emphasize this and to focus the discussion heavily into these one or two key positive areas. Do this to head off any damaging confrontations which might get out of proportion as a half dozen or so lesser issues, on which you have wide disagreement, get ironed out.

3. *Have any significant risks been surfaced?* Does this buyer appear to be credible and ethical? Do they intend to use our product or property or service for what it was designed? Or do they appear to have something in mind which may result in damages, claims, and costly hassles? Does it appear we could be opening ourselves to risks as accessories to regulatory or safety hazards? Have we given our

attorneys or our legal department sufficient inputs to permit a meaningful legal opinion? Have we adequately explored any other areas of potential risk that the buyer organization seemed to have alluded to during the discussion? And not least, do we have current and valid credit information on them; i.e., will they pay us—on time?

4. *Have we pushed them too far?* Have we overused our strength and boxed them into a corner which could backfire on us? Have we unnecessarily assured a deadlocked negotiation? What things can we do to remove the pressure without making major concessions? Should we gracefully back off a bit? Would it help to change negotiators, take a break, share some additional information with them, or make a minor concession?

5. *Are we prepared to resist late-hour pressure?* One of the biggest pitfalls in sales negotiations is the giving in to pressure when we sense the negotiation is getting down to the wire. This results in unnecessarily large concessions as perceived deadline pressures mount. Are we prepared to stick with a high target level and risk a deadlock? What happens if we do deadlock—will there be an opportunity to resume the negotiation later? Have we revised our minimum acceptable targets based on rational information, or are we bending to non-rational factors? What pressures are our negotiating opponents under in their organization? What cards have we held back and when should we play them? Resist, resist, resist!

6. *How can we avoid just splitting the difference?* A clever buyer may suggest that to get things wrapped up, why not just split the difference. "Charlie, this $3,000 worth of breakage is because of your crummy packaging, but I'm willing to split it with you if we can agree to it right now, 'cause I need the cash.'" You suspect the breakage was due to his own crummy handling equipment, but you can't prove it, and splitting the difference seems like a reasonable way out. But you could be setting a precedent, right? What happens if we hold to our guns and don't concede? What if we offer to pay 10%, "which is high, even for normal breakage allowances?" It is not a good deal to automatically split a difference. Nor is it good to cop out by striking some simple "average." The only time those measures are good deals is if the value of the time it will save you will be greater than any additional substantive value you might save by negotiating something better than an even split or a simple average. Indeed, an offer to split the difference is an opportunity to negotiate.

7. *What add-ons should we be alert to?* There are two sides to this. What freebies may the buyer ask for? What freebies might we ask for? Anything about minor design changes that could get thrown in right at the end after the basic sale has been agreed to? Shipping and

delivery always offers a variety of opportunities. Let's not get caught off base in a mood of victory as the sale is sealed. What kinds of add-on services might they try to slip in on us, and what equal or better add-ons could we ask for in response? Those little add-ons are right off the top of your net profit, so be oh so careful right at the end.

8. *Do any egos need attention?* Have there been any sensitive exchanges during the course of the negotiation which might suggest the need for some ego stroking before pushing for final agreement? Are there some positive things you can do or say which may help the other side feel good about what they are committing to? Have any egos in your own organization been at all bruised? Are those bruised persons critical to fulfilling the commitment? What kinds of things can you do to repair any such bruises in your own organization? Are there any background support types in the other organization who may feel their needs or inputs have been ignored? Is your key negotiating opponent under great pressure within his organization to come out of this looking very good? What might you be able to do to help him in this respect without jeopardizing your own position? Are there any ticklish areas you should be anticipating as things draw to a close, where great care must be taken to avoid damaging some egos on either side? Would it be useful to talk any of this through with your own team members before final commitment? Are there some egos which will simply have to be bruised in order to arrive at a satisfactory conclusion—if so, what can be done afterwards to minimize any long-term adversity?

9. *What benefits are there in summarizing the benefits?* After all, it's simply good basic salesmanship to summarize the benefits at the close of a sale. So why not do it at the close of a negotiation? Like closing a sale you wouldn't jeopardize gaining the commitment by spending a lot of valuable time summarizing the benefits your opponent should expect to realize—unless doing that may benefit you. Right? Well in a negotiation it might be useful to summarize some benefits to your opponent prior to tackling the final, and maybe most difficult, item on which you need commitment. If he is put into a positive mood, he might just be that bit more conciliatory—just enough to push him over the hump. It bears repeating, however hard a bargain you are driving, it is usually wise to make the other party feel some satisfaction. So summarize any benefits he's going to realize from the commitments he's making. If you have gained a price level which is obviously in your favor, stress the value he's receiving. If you have gained the short-term advantage, remind him of some long-term benefits to his organization. After all, it might be a long-term benefit to your organization if their organization realizes some long-term

benefits, especially if they feel that you are committed to helping them realize such benefits.

10. *How will you summarize actions on key agreements?* It's useful to do it visually; just to make sure what you said is what they understood and vice versa. Visually can mean the use of a detailed written summary or a detailed preliminary set of drawings, like blueprints. But in addition, it is often helpful to have some easy-to-digest slides or flipcharts or the like to point to so that everybody in the room is looking at the same item at the same time, while you're summarizing it. Especially if there is a lot of detailed legal or technical information, it's usually worth the time to summarize it in simple terms before putting any signature on that final commitment. That is, unless you are purposely trying to disguise some win-lose tactic in a snow of legal or technical mumbo-jumbo. That may lead to later hassles and delays when it's time for the "agreed upon" action to be taken. So if you are truly using mumbo-jumbo as a diversionary type tactic, it is wise to anticipate delays on agreed actions. The point is, it is desirable to summarize who has agreed to do what, when, and where—as a final checklist action, just prior to sealing the commitments. In very complex negotiations this summary of actions agreed to can take a bit of time, for it's when oftentimes a great deal of clarification of language and details takes place. If not conducted in a positive vein, focusing on key points step-by-step, many irrelevant tangents will be chased. And like every other step in the negotiation, it should be prepared for with a little bit of planning.

11. *How do you ask for the commitment?* Just ask for it—of course! Only, be careful you don't cave-in to one last demand by the buyer just to seal the commitment. Have a counter-demand ready in your hip pocket just in case. For instance, he says, "Okay Charlie, I think we've got a deal, if you can just do us one more favor by delivering half the shipment to our warehouse in Houston." A quick mental calculation tells you that request is filled with hidden costs, since you've already agreed to pick up the transportation charges. But you have to wrap this deal up within the next few minutes, because your buyer has another important meeting to go to. "Sure, Pat, we can do that and just bill you the difference on the transportation charges. Or if you'd rather, we could ship that part of the order to you here a couple weeks early so you can batch it with your next shipment to Houston."

    It's maybe not so important how you ask for the commitment (as long as it's firm and positive and all that) as it is to be prepared to deal with last-minute pressures which could weaken your position.

12. *Getting Closure on Details.* Hallelujah! The negotiation is over. Everybody has won, and the contract has been signed. Your job has been

completed and now it is up to the people back in production or service to carry the ball, right? Not so quick there, Charlie. To get agreement from the buyer, there were probably just a few little details you didn't discuss so as not to delay the successful conclusion. This was not because of oversight, nor was it an attempt at sidestepping. But very legitimately there are usually some details which were not directly related to the main agreement, but which need to be attended to in order that commitments are met as intended. Things like, "Okay, I'll have this contract typed up and have your two copies in the mail tomorrow morning." Or, "Jack will send the modified blueprints to your Engineering Supervisor on Friday." Or, there are a hundred and one follow-through details which need just as close attention as did the skillful maneuvering in the face-to-face negotiation. Negotiating has three critical phases: preparation, face-to-face bargaining, and follow-through, and the successful sales negotiator has a vital role in all three.

Checklist for Gaining Commitment

In major sales negotiations it is useful for you, and any of your negotiating partners, to review the following points before reaching final agreement. Even in a short, routine negotiation, a mental check of these will help.

- Do we really want to reach this agreement on these terms?
- What are the key issues as we near conclusion?
- Have any significant risks been surfaced?
- Have we pushed the buyers too far?
- What can we do to resist last-minute pressures?
- How can we avoid just "splitting the difference?"
- What "little" add-ons might the buyers request?
- Whose egos need some attention as we close?
- What benefits should be summarized to the buyers?
- What actions on key agreements need to be summarized?
- How will we ask for the commitment?
- On which details must we get closure?

Sales Manager: "Jean, my compliments. Great job you did negotiating! Next year's contract is the best arrangement we've ever had with Itex."

Sales Rep: "Well, thank you very much."

Rate Yourself on Your Skills at Gaining Commitment

How effective are you in gaining the best commitment possible in the late stages of your sales negotiations?

- Keeping both the substantive and the psychological issues in balance as you approach final agreement.
- Recognizing when deadlock is preferable to agreement.
- Avoiding diversions and pitfalls on minor issues.
- Dealing with new risks which have surfaced.
- Resisting concession pressures near the close.
- Anticipating add-ons the buyer may request after agreement is reached.
- Dealing with sensitive egos, on both sides, at the close.
- Raising the buyer's satisfaction by summarizing benefits.
- Summarizing "actions agreed to" from your perspective.
- Asking for the commitment on your terms.
- Getting closure on sticky details.

Sales Manager:	"Let's spend a few minutes just pinning down some follow-through."
Sales Rep:	"Okay. Good idea."
Sales Manager:	"Both legal and engineering have approved everything. Right?"
Sales Rep:	"Yes, and both have signed copies of all the final documents."
Sales Manager:	"Good. Now how about both purchasing and operations at Itex? Do they have signed copies as well as warranty details?"
Sales Rep:	"Yes, and this time our own customer service people have copies of the exceptions agreed to."
Sales Manager:	"Excellent. Can you think of anybody else either here, or at Itex, who needs to be tuned-in?"
Sales Rep:	"Only Sam in distribution. I sat down with Sam and the others over there, and we drafted a detailed schedule. We sent a copy to both purchasing and operations at Itex. Otherwise I think everything is nailed down."
Sales Manager:	"Thanks again, Jean, for an outstanding negotiation."

DOCUMENTING AGREEMENT AND ACTIONS

In most cases the matter of documenting the agreements reached in a sales negotiation is not all that complicated. It's often simply a matter of revising the items in the sales proposal or contract which have been negotiated, and sending the new or revised document to the person with whom you reached agreement. It's useful to double-check any such document against a "who, what, when, where, how, and extent or degree" set of questions to assure it covers the fundamental bases, but that should precede the final handshake and signatures in any case.

Naturally, it's important to make sure the appropriate people, and standard record-keeping functions, in your own organization have received copies of the agreement or contract. Company policies and procedures may dictate this, but you and your boss may need to decide who else in the organization needs copies to assure a good follow-through effort in fulfilling your side of the bargain.

But as with so many other things, 80% of your problems arise from only 20% of your negotiations. Thus the straightforward documenting of an agreement which suffices in most cases is not adequate in those few cases which somehow seem to generate all the follow-through difficulties. Therefore, at the risk of overkill, let's address some of the additional documentation considerations you should think about in more complex, or more unique, contracts and agreements. One way of protecting against downstream difficulties in any agreement is to consider the different parts of the buyer organization (as well as your own) whose actions will be critical to the satisfaction gained by both sides with this agreement, as well as with hoped for future business. To do this, let's categorize the types of people in the buyer's organization who may have impact. There are generally three types of influencers: (1) the actual *user* of your product or service—e.g., their production department, (2) the *technical* approver, and (3) the *management* approver. It is useful to consider what additional or special kinds of documentation each of these three types of influences may need to avoid roadblocks as the product or service you are providing goes into use in the buyer's organization.

How to Influence the User

The people in the buyer organization who are actually going to be using your product or service have some needs and motivations unique to them; i.e., not shared with the technical or managerial "approvers." For instance, a manufacturing plant may be less concerned with long-term financial implications, such as depreciation, than will be higher management. But the plant people will be far more concerned with ease of use and minimizing disruption of their daily work flow. The sales force may be far more interested in the comfort and styling of the car fleet you will be leasing them than the fellow in their leasing department who is responsible for minimizing maintenance costs and gas consumption. In other words, the different groups within the buyer organization who will be impacted by whatever you are selling or leasing them each have unique needs. And if any one group feels their needs have not been met, they may well exert enough pressure to curb the satisfaction and success of whatever you have successfully negotiated to provide. Then, not only is your current business apt to cost you more in servicing and responding to grievances, but future business could be in jeopardy.

Thus it is useful to think about what kind of information may be desirable to provide the "user" group in your buyer organization to assure that they understand how best to use your product or service to gain the advantages they are seeking. If the production people do not understand how to apply your product or service effectively, then not only will they not gain maximum benefits from its usage but also problems will arise, costly claims may develop, and all your skillful negotiating will be for naught. To head off this kind of pitfall, some clear "applications" data should be provided the "users," in language and format that they will *use* and *understand*. Otherwise, your next negotiation with that buyer may be over a claim rather than over future business.

During the sales negotiation, you may well have stressed all the usage and applications benefits of your product or service. The problem is you may not have been negotiating with the people on the firing line who will actually be using the information. So it's worth pausing after the negotiation is concluded to think about what kinds of information the "users" might need to cement-in their satisfaction with the benefits your product or service offers. Provide something that ties together your understanding of the users' objectives to the benefits you wish to stress. For if they have not been directly involved in the negotiating and some little problems arise later, end-user dissatisfaction can become costly to you.

Closely related to providing adequate applications and benefits information to the actual user is the issue of clearly stated "is-nots" about the usage of your product or service. Not to arouse negatives, but it is important that misuse be avoided through clearly stated instructions as to the kinds of things an uninformed user might typically try to do with your product, uses for which it was never designed—or risk dissatisfaction, possible claims and jeopardize future negotiations.

Another important part of "user" information is a statement of details or instructions regarding your follow-through commitments to them. Facts about your servicing policies and procedures, how to contact the right people in your organization for assistance, etc. is all a part of assuring a win-win result to a successful negotiation.

Some of the more typical end-users in a buyer organization whose specialized information needs should be considered are:

- *Production and Manufacturing*—the purchasing department may conduct the live negotiation for raw materials, semi-finished goods or capital equipment, and a higher level line executive may have approved the purchase agreement, but the front line supervisor is the one who needs clear information regarding use or application.

- *Sales and Marketing*—a line executive may have negotiated with you for a large sales promotion program, but it is his sales representatives who need some easy-to-use information as to how they can best apply your sales promotion package to their efforts.

- *Staff Groups*—your product or service may require applications understanding by any number of groups; e.g., engineering, computer services, accounting, personnel, etc. It is the astute sales negotiator who clearly determines how each of these groups will be using or depending upon the product or service, and assures that each receives the appropriate information.

- *Third Parties*—subcontractors, industry standards people, government agencies, parent company staff departments, and even customers of your customer, may become future pitfalls if they have not been given useful applications documentation. Not to overkill, but at least think through who else may genuinely need some clear information about how your negotiated package is (and is not) to be used.

Influencing the Technical Approver

This type may be located in your prospective buyer's engineering department, purchasing department, research or testing labs, quality control section, in a line function, a staff function, or goodness knows where in the organization. It behooves you to identify the technical approvers early-on in your negotiating so as to provide them with the detailed specifications, drawings, blueprints, or whatever they feel they need to pass positive judgment on your proposal. Indeed, if you can get to this type early enough, it's possible to get your proposal details written into their specifications and recommendations, to the extent of eliminating many would-be competitors from the bidding. And for the sake of support in future business, it may be useful to provide these types with follow-up information at the close of the negotiation, just to keep them on your side. This is not always necessary or desirable, but it's always worth thinking through.

"Could it enhance future business?" or "Could I head off possible resistance?" are questions you often need to ask yourself in terms of providing follow-through documentation to the "technical" approvers in the buyer organization. In providing such information, it is useful to give recognition to those technical people by referring to their inputs and recommendations, and linking the final outcome to their suggestions. If any of their specifications have been negotiated away, care must be taken to indicate why and how performance will be assured to their satisfaction—that is, unless certain issues are so sensitive as to be best left alone until results are proven.

In grooming the buyers' "technical" people in advance, and in building longer-term relationships following the negotiation, effective documentation is vital. To determine just what that effective documentation should consist of, it's desirable to consider what forces may be impacting the technical types. What government regulatory compliance issues concern them? Are there separate federal, state, and local compliance concerns? Are they thinking about not only current regulations but future possibilities as well? What industry associations guidelines are they expecting to follow? Are they complying with any standards bodies with which your organization is not familiar? How well thought out are their own performance specifications? It may be useful to consider these and many other questions in determining what information, both before and after the negotiation, will be useful in getting the "technical" approvers on your wavelength.

Influencing the Management Approver

By management approver, we mean the person whose signature, or whose verbal okay to go ahead and sign it, is the final step by the buyer organization to accept the purchase or contract. Of course that one individual may rely on other management kinds of approvers for advice before giving the final okay. For instance, if the Director of Operations is the one who must sign your purchase agreement, he may well seek advice from the finance department or from the cost analysts or from the people who analyze capital expenditures. He may need an internal approval from his purchasing department, or from some other executive who is responsible for corporate policies or longer-term financial considerations.

Do a bit of homework and probing to determine who these "management" approvers are, then assure that the kind of information which will help persuade them is made available to them. The responsible line executive for instance, may want a good overall grasp; hence, copies of all types of documentation are directed to each user, technical person, and management approver. Or, this overall perspective role may be in the hands of the responsible purchasing department manager. The type of discipline from which the approving manager hails does affect the emphasis of the kinds of information you will provide. Whomever it is, he or she needs a broad overview, but the particular orientation may vary in subtle ways.

If, for example, it's an executive with a financial background, he or she will be more particular about a well-prepared set of financial data (including key assumptions) than one without in-depth financial knowledge. Thus, it may warrant you're soliciting assistance from your own financial people in preparing that part of your proposal and follow-up information. This may seem obvious, but so often proposals and documentation are put together according to the same old format without regard to the type of person who will ultimately need to give management approval to the negotiated agreement. Again, let's stress, we're not talking just about the sales proposal, but the documenting of the final agreement or contract above and beyond just the wording of the contract or sales agreement itself. Taking it a step further, give consideration to all the backup information which you judge will be useful in helping that buyer to fulfill his side of the bargain and draw him closer to a long-term relationship with your organization.

Does their legal department have to approve the negotiated agreement? If so, should your legal department review the wording before it's presented in final form?

What kinds of documentation might help their purchasing department move the approval expeditiously through their approval channels? What other staff departments in their organization may need some additional information to put them at ease?

Are there any "third parties" involved in the approval? Any consultants or outside design firms who might have some specialized documentation requirements?

Tailoring the Follow-Through Information

There are people and groups in both your organizations who may impact the negotiation. In many cases, these groups need specialized information to meet their needs. It may be more detailed in some cases or a more simplified overview in others. If these groups do not get the clear picture they feel they need, either before agreement is reached, or in how to use your product and service after the sale is made, their dissatisfaction can undermine all your good negotiating efforts. It's useful to think of the types of groups who may need specialized information in terms of their "approval" role—that is, user, technical, or managerial. Granted, in many sales negotiations, one person fills all three roles, particularly in smaller buyer organizations. But think it through, for a little tailoring to individual needs can offer big payoff in the area of providing useful documentation during and after the sales negotiation.

FOLLOW-THROUGH INFORMATION WORKSHEET

After the completion of each negotiation think through who in each organization needs follow-through information or documentation to assure satisfaction and commitments by all parties involved. List under each category the information to be provided.

THEIR PEOPLE	OUR PEOPLE
Purchasing:	Sales Management:
Users:	Manufacturing:
Technical/Engineering:	Customer Service:
Management:	Distribution/Transportation:
Other:	Credit:
	Other:

Rate Yourself on Your
Attention to Follow-Through
Documentation and Information

How effective are you at providing key parties on both sides with follow-through information and documentation?

- Assuring commitment and follow-through in your own organization by providing appropriate information and documentation to key internal people.

- Determining who the users, technical approvers, and management approvers are in the buyer organization.

- Determining the exact kind of information needed by each key party in the buyer organization.

- Providing applications and benefits information to the actual "users" in the buyer organization.

- Providing appropriate information and documentation to the technical people in the buyer organization.

- Providing appropriate information to key management people in the buyer organization.

- Providing complete and accurate documentation to the purchasing department in the buyer organization.

- Identifying and fulfilling information/documentation needs of any third parties (agencies, consultants, etc.).

- Identifying any other parties who may need information or documentation to protect the contract or agreement.

- Maintaining accurate records of who needs and who has received, information and documentation of the agreement.

11

BUILDING RELATIONSHIPS FOR FUTURE NEGOTIATIONS

Sales Manager:	"James, it's been three months since you negotiated that contract with Columbus. How have things been going?"
Sales Rep:	"Pretty good, so far. Columbus had forgotten to include a key specification, but we were able to modify the equipment at no cost to us. They were surely relieved."
Sales Manager:	"That should help us next time around with them."
Sales Rep.	"It even helped us this time around. They had been giving one of our key competitors 30 percent of their supplies orders. Just to have a second source you know. After we bailed them out on the specification problem, they increased our share from 70% to 80%."
Sales Manager:	"Good show."
Sales Rep:	"It also gave us a chance to get our service people into their shop. It's amazing some of the information they've been able to gather in there."
Sales Manager:	"I hope you're keeping it all noted down for next year's contract."
Sales Rep:	"We have already started putting together our negotiating plan for next time around."
Sales Manager:	"Great."

BUILDING RELATIONSHIPS FOR FUTURE NEGOTIATIONS

Earlier, we observed that there are three stages in a sales negotiation: preparation, face-to-face, and follow-through. We examined the first two stages in detail. The third, and often most neglected stage, particularly as it completes a loop leading into future negotiations, is this business of follow-through.

As a super sales negotiator, you might feel that the primary burden of coordinating the delivery or installation of whatever you've sold is now up to your service or production or distribution department. After all, you have other potential customers to begin negotiating with. That's all true, but clearly the role of the sales professional goes beyond just staying in touch. And for very good reason. There may well still be additional opportunities for some give-and-take, even on the negotiation that has been formally completed.

Keep in mind that a skilled buyer is still looking for value to be gained—in the form of asking for little additional services, replacements for items which purportedly haven't passed "his" quality control, and so on. To deal effectively with these requests, you should be prepared to negotiate tradeoffs in the form of requesting little favors in return from the buyer—favors which will add, or salvage, some value for the seller, while maintaining and building a stronger long-term relationship in anticipation of future business.

Making Modifications and Refinements

One area to be alert to, as the stuff you've sold begins to get used by the buyer, has to do with errors and oversights. However painstakingly both sides have done their homework, that "lousy computer" can still slip a blip, and somehow it doesn't get discovered until the buyer begins actually using your product or service. It doesn't really matter whose "computer" it was that goofed. Your buyer now has a problem and expects you to help him salvage some value. Your objective then is to help satisfy him but to avoid costing your own organization any significant value. You do this by generating some set of tradeoffs which are acceptable to the buyer, but which either prevents you from incurring any significant costs, or replaces them with other value gained.

In addition to the necessity of "renegotiating" errors and oversights which may crop-up, the occasional misunderstanding may also arise whereby the customer says: "No, I didn't mean FOB 'your' plant,

I meant FOB 'our' plant"—or other such fun items. After you've counted to ten you have three choices: concede—blow the next order—or renegotiate.

Then, there are those questions which come up afterward. They don't involve errors, oversights, or misunderstandings, but nevertheless they do require some clarification and perhaps some further negotiation. "Well Charlie, could you clarify how we can meet these regulatory requirements of *our* customers when we are using the process we bought from you?" There may not be any way they can meet those other regulatory requirements without bearing some extra costs. But you may be able to help share some of their costs, "if you could help us out with the following—."

There is also the issue of unforeseen developments which occur after your sale has been negotiated, signed, sealed, and consummated—but before the products or services have been delivered to the buyer. For instance, you may have been hit with a major equipment failure, an unexpected labor difficulty, or some other event which will seriously impair your ability to meet the terms of the contract. Prepare to negotiate! Plan a series of tradeoffs which will satisfy your buyer's needs but which will minimize your own losses.

Unexpected opportunities may also arise after your negotiation is officially completed. Whether the opportunity would be primarily to your good fortune or mostly for the buyer, for goodness sake, take advantage of it. Practically any contract is renegotiable if it makes sense for both the seller and the buyer, so look for the win-win tradeoffs and renegotiate.

On the flip-side, unanticipated problems will naturally occur, problems which neither you nor your buyer could have predicted. It would be shortsighted for either side in a long-term business relationship to refuse to renegotiate some relief for the other party when such problems arise. Maybe the buyer's specs were too loose, and although your product is within contract specification, his equipment cannot process it properly. Whatever the problem, it isn't necessarily just a matter of absorbing additional costs to help bail him out. It can very well be an opportunity to re-explore tradeoffs discussed first time around and to look for new ones.

ANOTHER LOOK AT CLIMATE

Back in Chapter 5 we examined the importance of establishing the appropriate climate in a sales negotiation. In a one-shot deal, with the "get as good a price as you can" buyer, you may judge that a win-lose is unavoidable. In that case, stage 3 or the follow-through part of the negotiation, is usually minimized since it is not your intent to work with that buyer on a continuing basis. But most sales negotiations should be on a win-win basis. Even if you won't be negotiating with that particular buyer in the near future, you are looking at the word-of-mouth value his satisfaction will be to your business in the future.

It's always useful to look at what we call the Negotiating Climate Quadrant, in terms of climate implications. So let us look at the following Quadrant with that in mind. Note that a lose-lose would rarely occur unless both sides were terribly obstinate or some unexpected and unfortunate events occurred to submarine an otherwise fruitful negotiation. Also note that on this Quadrant, each side can pull against the other ultimately winding up in a win-lose, but if the two sides cooperate and look for tradeoff opportunities, a win-win can be achieved with no loss in overall value to either side.

Seller Win Buyer Lose			Seller Win Buyer Win
	Selling Price Only	Areas of Opportunity in other trade-offs, e.g. transportation, service, payment terms, specs, etc.	
Seller Value	Refusal to Negotiate	Offering Price Only	
Seller Lose Buyer Lose		*Buyer Value*	Buyer Win Seller Lose

The Negotiating Climate Quadrant

Now you may be asking, "But how about that business of Lose-Win mentioned back in Chapter 6, where does that fit in?" Well remember, in Chapter 6 we were viewing the negotiation from the seller's perspective primarily, whereas the above quadrant is an overall perspective—seller and buyer. In that respect a lose-win from the seller's perspective would show up on this Quadrant as a Buyer Win-Seller Lose. In Chapter 5, that was offered as a temporary situation the seller might resort to, to help bail the buyer out of difficulty for the sake of long-range mutual benefit.

And really, that's one of the key points for consideration here in the issue of renegotiating errors, oversights, misunderstandings, clarifications, new developments, opportunities, and problems, after the original negotiation has been consummated. Will it be useful to you to suffer a temporary lose-win by offering to renegotiate a difficulty, for the sake of long-range satisfaction? So lose-win, as a conscious decision on the part of the seller may indeed fit in, even in stage 3, or the follow-through part of a sales negotiation. It's important to observe, however, that a lose-win outcome, temporarily accepted by either side to help the other out of a difficulty, is actually a strategy within a longer range win-win climate.

Clearly a win-win climate achieved during a sales negotiation should be sustained in the follow-through stage if future business is a possibility. A more interesting point is the question of attempting to build a win-win climate during the follow-through stage of a negotiation which wound up as a win-lose. In this case, each sale and each contract must be looked at on its own merits and if future business is a possibility, then some cooperation and some long-range relationship building may well be warranted.

ASSURING FOLLOW-THROUGH ACTIVITIES

We've looked at follow-through issues in terms of dealing with new problems and opportunities which arise after the negotiation is completed. But new factors aside, there are some standard things which should always be done, particularly in team negotiations, to build those relationships for future negotiations.

Follow-through attention to the recent sale should be used as a bridge into that buyer organization to learn as much as possible about their operations, their people, and their way of doing things. Get your technical people talking with their technical people, to help learn as much as possible about them and to begin gathering useful information which will be helpful in planning your next negotiation with them or with similar buyers. This business of "getting inside" the buyer organization is also an opportunity for you and your people to begin grooming their people to support you by recommending your product or service when they begin planning their next round of negotiations.

Some of the most common mistakes, and the failure to seize new opportunities, fall into this general area of getting your own sales organization people effectively involved in follow-through activities with the buyer organization with the objective of preparing for the future. The following are the five key pitfalls an effective sales negotiator will be constantly on top of throughout the negotiation follow-through:

1. *Failure to research the buyer organization.* Follow-through "service calls" should always be used to gather intelligence about possible tradeoffs in future negotiations. There are always possible concessions and counter-concessions you may ask for next time around if you systematically look for them—beforehand.

2. *Failure to build your team early enough.* There may be many people within your organization who should be "tuned in" to help you prepare for the next sales negotiation with a given buyer. Get them organized during that follow-through stage and give each of them some objectives as to the types of information they might gather, the ways they may help groom key people in the buyer organization, and what not to say in terms of giving away future bargaining strength. There is no better time to start building your team for a future negotiation than during the follow-through stage of your last one.

3. *Giving away future bargaining strength.* It's one thing to share salient information in a cooperative way in a win-win relationship, but it's quite another to give away unnecessary information, especially if it gives the buyer some concessions to ask for next time around. The problem arises in the follow-through stage of a successful negotiation when you or your people, in the enthusiasm of cooperation, let slip some new developments, or some anticipated difficulties with your product, that tips off the buyer to some bargaining vulnerabilities you may have. Things like, "Oh boy, we've come up with a new process to lower our manufacturing costs by 30%." Your buyer will surely see this as an opportunity to ask for a reduced price next negotiation. And it is information not really necessary for your assisting him in any of his applications or installation or servicing of his present contract with you. Avoiding this pitfall is closely related to your team building efforts; i.e., keeping everybody from your organization, who is in touch with that buyer, tuned-in as to what not to say in conversations with their people.

4. *Failure to groom the buyer's organization.* This again, is closely related to your own team building. If you can get their people to write the

unique aspects of your product into their specifications, formally or informally; if you can get critical information about their future bargaining points; if you can just get their key people to prefer doing business with your organization—you're on your way to a successful negotiation next time around.

5. *Failure to plan.* The foundation for avoiding the first four pitfalls is planning. What better time to plan for your next negotiation with Buyer A than during your follow-through efforts on the last negotiation with Buyer A. Only through good planning will you know what intelligence you need to start gathering about them, what the likely "team" makeup will be, what information your side needs to protect, and what strategies are likely to be most effective in "grooming" them for the next round of negotiations.

OFFERING RELIEF

Earlier we talked about the idea of helping out a buyer who had been hit with an unexpected problem. We touched on a similar issue in terms of accepting a temporary lose-win—i.e., short-term sacrifice—to foster a long-range win-win climate with the buyer. The whole idea is that in long-range relationships with buyers, negotiating isn't confined to the specific face-to-face sale of a given contract or purchase, but the give-and-take extends throughout your entire business relationship with that buyer.

Just to turn the tables for a moment, if you've agreed to sell ten units of Product X to Buyer A, but before you were able to ship it, Buyer B got into a pinch and very badly needed five of those units of Product X which were intended for Buyer A, it would be nice if you could go to Buyer A and explain the situation and get his okay to delay half his order so you could satisfy Buyer B. Well that is far more apt to work out to your satisfaction if Buyer A has confidence that when he gets into a bind, he could count on you to offer him some relief; i.e., to reciprocate.

The payoff in showing a willingness to offer some kind of relief to a buyer who's in trouble will not be limited to that buyer alone. If word gets around the industry that although you are a skilled negotiator you are a win-win negotiator, that you will give and take, and give relief after the negotiation when it is really justified, then you will be gaining, not sacrificing, future negotiating strength.

This is not to promote cream-puff-ism amongst sales negotiators. Note we said offer relief when it is justified, not every time it's requested. There are buyers who make a career of shouting for relief every time their people or their equipment make a mess of whatever you've sold them. Giving in to invalid claims of bad product or poor service is not smart negotiating, and only diminishes long-term strength.

The difficulty, of course, is in all those gray areas when neither side is very sure what caused your product or service not to work out, where you are willing to negotiate some relief, but not all they are seeking. That is when you reapply all the negotiating planning and strategies and skills already discussed within the framework of whichever long-range climate you wish to maintain.

PLANNING FOR THE FUTURE

Negotiating with buyer organizations is often a continuing process. It does not end the moment the contract or sales order is signed.

Regarding buyers with whom we expect to be doing business in the future, the effectiveness with which we negotiate on follow-through requests, service, disagreements over claims, or returned goods, and all the support items they may ask for while using our product or service, is just as critical to our long-term revenues and profits as negotiating the original sale. The sales negotiator who does not have net profits in mind as a primary objective can easily "give away the store" after the sale is made. For every concession the buyer requests in that follow-through stage, we must be prepared to ask for something in return.

This all suggests that next time you are planning for a negotiation, build into that plan, those areas of concession which might come up after the sale is made. A negotiation plan should cover all the things you need to do in all three stages of the negotiation—the before, the during, and the after.

Now that all three stages of the negotiation have been considered, go back over the planning format, and the planning steps, to analyze the thoroughness of your own preparations for a forthcoming negotiation. And for goodness sake, don't do it in a vacuum. Bounce your plan off somebody else—another salesperson, a boss, or a key support person—to get their insights and inputs into your preparations.

Negotiating with regular customers and long-term accounts never ends. It is a continuous cycle (see Negotiating Cycle on Page 168) of planning, negotiating, then follow-through—during which the planning for next go-round begins all over again. For this reason, each of the three stages is of equal significance and throughout it all, the importance of team, or organizational effectiveness, is paramount.

THE NEGOTIATING CYCLE

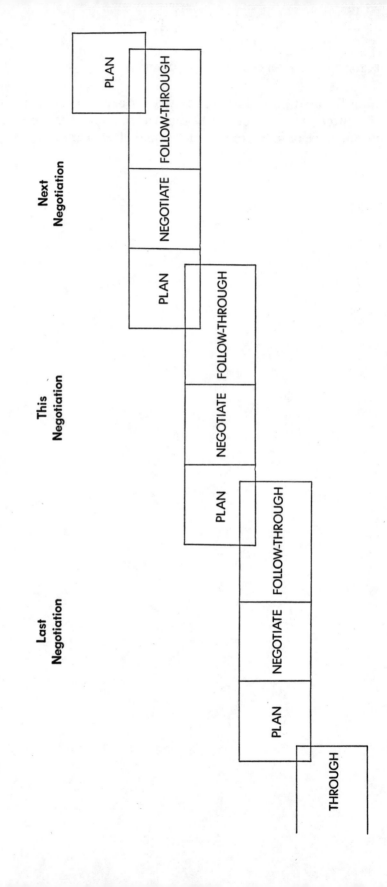

Rate Yourself on Your Attention to Follow-Through

How effective are you at negotiations follow-through?

- Recognizing give-and-take opportunities following a completed negotiation.
- Renegotiating errors, oversights, and misunderstandings.
- Enhancing a win-win climate following the negotiation.
- Keeping the long-range perspective in mind.
- Keeping the right people in your organization involved in the "negotiating" aspects of follow-through.
- Continually "researching" the buyer organization for negotiations enhancements.
- Building your own negotiating team for the next negotiation during the follow-through on this one.
- Protecting future bargaining strength.
- Grooming the buyer's organization for future negotiations.
- Providing relief to the buyer who has gotten into a bind after your negotiation is over.
- Beginning your planning for the next negotiation during follow-through on this one.

CHECKLIST FOR
BETTER SALES NEGOTIATIONS

Friend:	"I understand you've just finished a rather important negotiation with one of your key customers."
Sales Rep:	"Sure did."
Friend:	"Who won?"
Sales Rep:	"We both won."
Friend:	"How about that."

A CHECKLIST FOR BETTER SALES NEGOTIATIONS

For a negotiation to take place, both the seller and the buyer must have the flexibility to agree to some tradeoffs or concessions. In most negotiations, the need to buy has already been established. The negotiation is the process for determining from which seller the buyer will purchase, at what levels, and under what conditions.

To engage in this process effectively, there are five areas of characteristics which are generally required of you, the salesperson. They are: a high goal orientation, effective preparation, good face-to-face skills, attention to follow-through, and a win-win perspective. To enhance an understanding of some of the specific things you need to consider in fulfilling these characteristics, the following list of 57 items is offered.

Planning the Sales Negotiation

1. Set our objective(s) as high as possible, within the realm of believability, before beginning our negotiating plan.

2. Develop a checklist of homework items; i.e., information we need to gather about our own tradeoff possibilities and about our prospective buyer organization.

3. Make a list of, and contact each person in our organization, who could be a valuable information resource or negotiating team member.

4. Lay out an Objectives Setting Worksheet similar to the one in Chapter 2.

5. Get some team members or support people to help make a list of assumptions, we may be making, which could be impacting our objectives and tradeoff possibilities.

6. Plan as carefully to conduct some internal negotiations as we do the external; i.e., the negotiation with the buyer.

7. List the internal commitments and tradeoffs I should negotiate with our own people before negotiating commitments with the buyer.

8. Check back with key people in our organization as conditions change and new information surfaces about the negotiation with the buyer.

9. Get somebody who understands more about cost, pricing, and financial issues, than I do, to talk us through those issues from both our viewpoint and the buyer's.

10. Make a list of what we think our prospective buyer's objectives will be in the negotiation.

11. Rough out an information grid similar to the one in Chapter 3.

12. Note down what kind of negotiating climate we'd like to wind up in at the close of the negotiation.

13. Also note down the kind of climate we think the buyer will start out in.

14. List some ways we will go about establishing the climate we expect to develop.

15. Now list some barriers we may encounter to establish that climate.

16. Make a list of our bargaining strengths and weaknesses and a list of our buyer's bargaining strengths and weaknesses.

17. Write down the negotiating strategy we intend to pursue.

18. List the tactics we plan to employ within that strategy.

19. List the tactics we expect the buyer to employ and our corresponding counter-tactics

20. List some self-discipline, or team-discipline, pitfalls which we may need to anticipate in this negotiation.

21. Prepare a description of informational items which must not be "leaked" before, during, or after the negotiation.

22. Brief any people in our organization who might be in a position to unwittingly leak that information as to the importance of not doing so.

23. Note down any ego-type factors which may test our (or our team members') negotiating disciplines during the bargaining.

Conducting the Face-to-Face Negotiation

24. Write out a very high opening demand (price, conditions, etc.), then ask ourselves why we can't raise it a bit higher—just for openers.

25. Conduct at least one or two role-plays with our own people, using that high opening demand, followed by the various strategies, tactics, and counter-tactics which might arise.

26. Offer rationale for our high demands.

27. Think through the worst kinds of responses and counter-offers the buyer may initially employ and how we will deal with that to keep the negotiation on a positive track.

28. Discuss with our team or support people any product or service credibility issues to be considered during the negotiation.

29. Consider any difficult questions the buyer could pose regarding my personal "credibility" as the key sales negotiator.

30. Note down how we plan to use any of the seven credibility tools described in Chapter 7.

31. What credibility "weaknesses" in the buyer organization might we use to gain concessions or counter-concessions?

32. What information gaps and assumptions in our original plan need to be filled-in, updated, or tested in the face-to-face meetings?

33. What "hidden agendas," if any, and unexpected information have we picked up during our initial face-to-face bargaining, and how does this modify our original plan?

34. Which of the eight rules in Chapter 6 are we employing to gather intelligence in the face-to-face meeting(s)?

35. What information gathering techniques does the buyer seem to be using, and how should we be responding?

36. Who are all the key people within the buyer organization, and what are their various interests in this negotiation?

37. Are there any internal conflicts within the buyer organization, and how can I best deal with them?

38. Which of our tactics appear to be working?

39. Which of our buyer's counter-tactics appear to be working, and what can we do to reduce them?

40. What unexpected tactics are being employed by the buyer and how should we be dealing with them?

41. Which of our own counter-tactics are, and are not, working—what modifications are needed, if any?

42. Are the tactics and counter-tactics we are using in concert with the negotiating climate we want to be in?

43. Is there any time pressure in this negotiation—if so, how should we be dealing with it?

44. What new opportunities have surfaced in this negotiation?

45. Should we change strategies or team makeup to better cope with a changing situation in this negotiation?

46. Have we refined the commitment we are seeking as we approach the conclusion of the negotiation, and is it still in our interests to reach an agreement with this buyer?

47. Can we gain some value by summarizing the key issues on which we have agreement before bearing down on the areas of difference?

48. What pressures and pitfalls may we need to deal with as we get down to the conclusion of this negotiation?

49. What final tactics and strategies are we going to employ to get closure on the best deal possible?

Follow-Through on the Negotiation

50. What basic documentation (of our negotiated agreement) needs to be finalized and who gets copies?

51. Does the actual "user" group in the buyer's organization need any additional information to assure their proper and effective use of our product or service?

52. Any additional information that would be useful to lock-in the "technical" approvers of the buyer's organization?

53. How about additional documentation—legal, financial, etc.—which might be of particular value in gaining points with the buyer's "management" approvers?

54. What future modifications, opportunities, or refinements issues might we anticipate after the sales agreement is concluded, and how will we renegotiate them?

55. Are we clear as to how we will renegotiate with the buyer if he has a problem and asks us for relief?

56. What other follow-through items do we need to attend to in assuring that the results of this negotiation turn out as intended?

57. As we follow-through this negotiation, what issues should we address which will help us in future negotiations with this same buyer?

Most commercial sales negotiations in which we are involved include some elements of both the win-win and the win-lose. Throughout, we have suggested the wisdom of considering the former as the dominant climate in long-range business relationships. Do not do this to the point of naively pursuing a win-win course while an aggressive buyer is taking you apart concession by concession. But adopt it as a general philosophy of negotiating.

In every negotiation, there is a degree of competition. Although over time a climate of seller-buyer cooperation in seeking innovative ways to benefit both sides is usually the most productive, not all buyers subscribe to that philosophy and not all situations permit it.

Whether your next negotiation is primarily cooperative or highly competitive, the above checklist should guide you through those thought processes so critical in the planning, conducting, and follow-through of an effective sales negotiation.

Rate Yourself on Your Overall Negotiating Skills

How effective are you at the total negotiating process?

- Setting high level goals.
- Planning effectively for your sales negotiations.
- Conducting the face-to-face negotiation.
- Assuring productive follow-through after each negotiation.
- Maintaining a win-win perspective throughout your sales negotiations.

BIBLIOGRAPHY

Fisher, Roger, and William Ury, *Getting to Yes*. Boston: Houghton-Mifflin, 1981.

Karrass, Chester L., *Give and Take*. New York: Thomas Y. Crowell Company, 1974.

Karrass, Chester L., *The Negotiating Game*. New York: Thomas Y. Crowell Company, 1970.

Karrass, Gary, *Negotiating to Close*. New York: Simon and Schuster, 1985.

Nierenberg, Gerard I., *The Art of Negotiating*. New York: Hawthorn, 1968.

Nierenberg, Gerard I., *Fundamentals of Negotiating*. New York: Hawthorn/Dutton, 1973.

Index

Concessions
  changing, 70
  commitments and, 146
  counter-tactics and, 134-35
  extras, 70, 139, 141
  matching, 46-47
  rate at which, are made, 71
  setting, 66-67
Contracts, preprinted, 102
Cost information, assembling, 36-37
Counter-offers, dealing with
  assumptions and, 84
  delays and, 85-86
  emotional managers and, 83
  large amounts of data and, 85
  offensive buyers and, 85
  pressure and, 84
  role of team members in, 83-84
  rush deadlines and, 85
  "sweet" buyers and, 84
  take-it-or-leave-it attitudes and, 84-85
  very low opening offers and, 83
  wrong negotiator and, 85
Counter-tactics
  authority levels and, 136-37
  in a balanced market, 131-32
  in a buyers' market, 131
  climate and, 130-31
  concessions and, 134-35
  ego attacks and, 137-38
  for extras, 139
  list of tactics and, 141
  purpose of, 140
  rating yourself on the use of, 142
  in a sellers' market, 132
  validity testing and, 139
Counter-tactics, preparing
  establish team roles, 74
  list buyer's likely tactics, 72-73
  preparing your, 73-74
  role play and, 74
Counter-tactics to use against buyer's tactics of
  authority levels and, 136-37
  ego attacks and, 137-38
  high opening demands, 134-35
  information barrages and voids, 135
  making changes in the package, 135-36
  team manipulations, 138-39
  time pressure, 132-34
  tough guy, 139
  using irrelevancies, 138

Credibility, establishing
  demonstrating person, 98-99
  example of, 97
  facts and statistics and, 100-101
  how to, 99-103
  importance of, 98
  laws and regulations and, 102-3
  policies and procedures and, 103
  precedents and, 103
  printed documents and labels and, 101-2
  rating yourself on, 106
  standard industry practice and, 100
  types of information that gets questioned, 99
  use of media for, 101
Credibility planner, 105

D

Deadlines
  countering, 133-34
  dealing with rush, 85
Deadlocks
  countering, 133, 141
  planned, 71, 93
Delay tactics, 85-86
Discipline
  avoiding pitfalls to effective, 44-48
  importance of, 43
  rating yourself on, 50
  in a win-win climate, 61
Diversions, dealing with, 138, 141
Documenting agreements and actions
  checking of, 151
  management approvers and, 155-56
  technical approvers and, 154-55
  users and, 152-54
Documents and labels, use of printed, 101-2

E

Ego(s)
  -building tactics, 72
  commitments and, 147
  counter-tactics and, 137-38, 141
  discipline, 47-48
  in a win-win climate, 60
Emotionalism
  managers and, 83
  use of, 134
Errors, dealing with, 160-61